Alexander John Ellis

Practical Hints on the Quantitative Pronunciation of Latin

For the Use of Classical Teachers and Linguists

Alexander John Ellis

Practical Hints on the Quantitative Pronunciation of Latin
For the Use of Classical Teachers and Linguists

ISBN/EAN: 9783337062705

Printed in Europe, USA, Canada, Australia, Japan

Cover: Foto ©Thomas Meinert / pixelio.de

More available books at **www.hansebooks.com**

QUANTITATIVE PRONUNCIATION
OF LATIN.

PRACTICAL HINTS ON THE

QUANTITATIVE PRONUNCIATION

OF LATIN.

FOR THE USE OF CLASSICAL TEACHERS AND LINGUISTS.

BY

ALEXANDER J. ELLIS, B.A., F.R.S., F.S.A., F.C.P.S., F.C.P.

Past President of the Philological Society,
Formerly Scholar of Trinity College, Cambridge,
Author of " Early English Pronunciation."

ἡ μὲν γὰρ πεζῇ λέξις οὐδενὸς οὔτ' ὀνόματος, οὔτε ῥήματος,
βιάζεται τοὺς χρόνους, οὐδὲ μετατίθησιν· ἀλλ' οἵας παρείληφε
τῇ φύσει τὰς συλλαβὰς τάς τε μακρὰς καὶ τὰς βραχείας,
τοιαύτας φυλάττει.

DION. HAL. First Century, B.C. (See Art. 41)

London:

MACMILLAN AND CO.

1874.

LONDON:

R. CLAY, SONS, AND TAYLOR, PRINTERS,

BREAD STREET HILL.

PRELIMINARY NOTICE.

PROF. ROBINSON ELLIS, of University College, London, at the close of the Report on Latin Philology which he was kind enough to contribute to my farewell presidential address to the Philological Society (delivered on May 15, 1874), introduced the subject of Latin Pronunciation as follows :—

"The question of Pronunciation forms one of the subjects discussed at the Schoolmasters' Conference this year. The meeting which was held early in 1871 at Oxford, to take steps for the reformed pronunciation of Latin, and the conference of schoolmasters held about the same time, resulted in the combined *Syllabus of Latin Pronunciation* drawn up by Professor Munro of Cambridge and Professor Palmer of Oxford. This was at once introduced into several of the larger schools in England, at least in the higher forms. I myself adopted it for the use of my classes in University College, and a very similar scheme of pronunciation was only last year printed by Professor Key for University College School. Independently of this, a reformed pronunciation has been adopted in various educational establishments in this country; and it is no uncommon occurrence in my classes to find students on their arrival already trained in the new method, with such slight differences (and they are really slight) as the divergence of opinion on particular points makes unavoidable. It would be premature at present to express any opinion as to the eventual success of this experiment; it can hardly be said as yet to have been adequately tried in schools, or properly seconded in the Universities. At Oxford, when I examined vīvā vōce as Classical Moderator in 1872, I was the only examiner who used the reformed pronunciation, and those who then came before me for examination did not generally seem familiar with it. Even now the old use predominates, and it is to be feared that even those trained by the Syllabus at school, *e.g.*, at Shrewsbury, Marlborough, Liverpool College, Christ's Hospital, Dulwich College and the City of London School, are induced to give it up, or, at least to suppress it, when they proceed to the Universities. On one point there seems to be a very general agreement : wherever it has been introduced, it has been adopted without difficulty by students of all ages, even by the youngest boys, from ten years old upwards. It is obvious that if it is to be really successful, it should be taught alone ; at present the old pronunciation is allowed to linger on side by side with the new. This would not happen if boys were trained at the outset on the new system, and if it were an understood thing that no other pronunciation was permitted. But the lamentable fluctuation of opinion exhibited by the schoolmasters in their conference of this year is a clear proof, if any proof were wanted, of the difficulties which invariably attend any real reform ; and it becomes doubly incumbent on institutions, which, like University College, and Owens College, Manchester, represent enlightened opinion irrespective of denomination, and which for that reason necessarily work independently, to devote their best energies to the successful carrying out of this apparently small, but in my judgment really important, detail." — *Transactions of the Philological Society*, 1873—4, pp. 398—9.

These remarks induced me to add some observations (*ibid*, pp. 399—407) in which I dwelt on the practical difficulties of making the change, and stated candidly that though I utterly abhorred the old English habit of Latin pronunciation I had been taught to use at Shrewsbury and Eton (1826—1833), yet that if schoolmasters sought success only by *written* examinations, it was hardly worth their while to make the change. And, I remarked, there was no use in disguising the fact that the change to be effective must be troublesome. There were really no difficulties for English speakers, I explained, in adopting the new sounds proposed for vowels and consonants. " The real trouble of the new pronunciation begins," I emphatically stated, " just where no trouble is suspected—in accent and quantity." I then shewed that though, as an Eton boy, I had been taught to feel a holy horror for " false quantities," yet also as an Eton boy, I had been perpetually making false quantities in common with all the Eton masters themselves. In *sīc vōs nōn vōbīs nīdificātis avēs*, it was usual, in my day, to pronounce *sīc* like English *sick*, *nōn* to rhyme with *on*, *vōbīs* with the last syllable like the first in *biscuit*, *nīdificātis* with the syllables as far as the *a* like English *nid″ifica′tion*, and *avēs* with *av* as in *aviary*, so that five false quantities were made in one short line. Of course *o′pus op′eris*, *sō′lus sōl′itūdo*, and the like, furnished thousands of others. Since the *place* of the Latin accent is dependent on the quantity of the last syllable but one, in words of more than two syllables, if the accent were placed right there, the speaker was held to have made no "false quantities;" and if in his verses he followed the laws in his "gradus" which were at utter variance with the custom of his speech, he was also held to have made no "false quantities." That he did not pronounce a single vowel correctly by intention, that he did not understand the nature of long and short vowels or syllables, or the rhythm that they made in verse (except as by "gradus" aforesaid), that he had no conception of what the nature of Latin accent was, and that Latin as he uttered it (not as he saw it) was pure *vōx et praetereā nihil*, sound without any sense at all to a Roman's ears,—of this he had no conception whatever, though in his ignorance he did not hesitate to laugh at a Frenchman's or German's English, which, however poor, would be at any rate properly intended, and at least intelligible.

Having, in view of opening this subject in the address already cited, made an arrangement with the College of Preceptors, to give them a paper on Latin Pronunciation at their monthly meeting in June, I purposely went into this particular question of Latin Accent and Quantity (and especially the latter as determining the former), in a practical paedagogical paper. The chair was occupied by the Rev. G. C. Bell, Head Master of Christ's Hospital, the largest school in England which, as previously mentioned by Prof. Robinson Ellis, has adopted the new sounds of the letters, and I had an audience of classical teachers, who during an address of unexampled length (nearly two hours and a half) listened with that attention which only great practical interest in the subject could command.

In revising this paper for separate publication, I have found it necessary to expand many parts, and in especial to add and interpret many passages from Cicero and Quintilian (the only authorities of any value), and to put in a much more complete form the arguments which have induced me to treat the (so-called) elided vowels and final M in the manner here advocated. But not to confuse the order of the exposition, I have relegated much of this accessory matter to footnotes. Finally I have endeavoured, as well as it was possible on paper, to convey a conception of the mode in which I read the examples, which form an Appendix at the close of this tract. I wish it had been possible for me to freeze up my utterances into some Munchausen's postboy's horn, so that my readers might have only had to hang it up in the ingle] and hear the very sounds which I have, I fear often vainly, tried to convey on paper. But I have given such ample practical directions for self-practice that I hope classical teachers and classical scholars, and linguists in general (for whom, and not for pupils, my book, and especially its notes, have been put together), who feel interest enough in the subject to undertake the labour, will be able to make Latin *live* again in themselves, and breathe its magic through their own lips into the souls of their hearers.

A. J. E.

June 27, 1874.
25 ARGYLL ROAD, KENSINGTON, W.

CONTENTS.

ERRATA.

p. 8, *l.* 4 *from bottom of note, read*: slackening strings

p. 27, *l.* 14 *from bottom of note, read:* μουσική

p. 46, *l.* 1 *read:* af·χrənd

p. 46, *l.* 10 and 11, read: *svāve svāvem*

p. 50, *l.* 5 *from bottom, read:* those considerations

p. 51, *l.* 5 *from top, read:* that *m*

p. 66, *l.* 1, read: *inaudible*

QUANTITATIVE PRONUNCIATION
OF LATIN.

I. Preliminary Assumptions.

ART. 1.—The object of this book is entirely practical. It is therefore necessary to make several assumptions, requiring for their justification much detailed consideration for which reference must in general be made to other treatises.[1]

[1] Not only the immense and, for scholars, indispensable treatise : Ueber Aussprache, Vokalismus und Betonung der Lateinischen Sprache von W. Corssen, 2te Auflage, Leipzig, 1863, Vol. I. pp. xvi. 819; Vol. II. pp. 1086, but the following more accessible English treatises :—
Syllabus of Latin Pronunciation drawn up at the request of the Head Masters of Schools. Cambridge and Oxford, 1872. 8vo. pp. 7.—A few remarks on the Pronunciation of Latin, with a postscript by H. A. J. Munro. Cambridge, 1871. 8vo. pp. 36.—A Grammar of the Latin Language, from Plautus to Suetonius, by Henry John Roby. Part I. 1st edition, 1871, sm. 8vo. pp. xcv., 476, of which at least 150 pages are devoted to pronunciation. 2nd edition, 1872, in which these remarks are enlarged, with replies to Prof. Munro's pamphlet just cited, etc.—The Public School Latin Grammar, for the Use of Schools, Colleges, and Private Students, by Benjamin Hall Kennedy, D.D. 2nd edition, 1874, pp. xxix., 599, of which at least 68 pages are devoted to phonology and its applications.—Elements of Latin Pronunciation for the Use of Students in Language, Law, Medicine, Zoology, Botany, and the Sciences generally in which Latin words are used, by S. S. Haldeman. Philadelphia, 1851. 8vo. pp. 76.—Latin Pronunciation, an inquiry into the proper sounds of the Latin language during the classical period, by Walter Blair, Professor of Latin in Hampden Sidney College, Virginia. New York and Chicago, 1873. 8vo. pp. 136, an extremely useful little work reviewed in the *Southern Magazine*, October, 1873, by Professor S. S. Haldeman, who refers also to—J. F. Richardson's Roman Orthoepy,

ART. 2.—First, I assume that sufficient interest has been recently excited both theoretically and practically in the question of Latin pronunciation, to make teachers and scholars willing to take a good deal of personal trouble to gain some insight into its nature as a living reality and not merely as a paper fiction.

ART. 3.—I assume that the utmost value which can be attributed to the current English pronunciation of Latin is, that it serves rather roughly to recall to Englishmen, and no one else, the letters with which the words are written in ordinary printed books.

ART. 4.—I assume that this same current English pronunciation is positively injurious even to Englishmen, who wish to understand the nature of Latin linguistically, its flexional and historical relations either as descendant or ancestor, and its rhythmical structure either oratorical or poetical.

ART. 5.—I assume that by Latin pronunciation we mean that current among the principal men of eminence as statesmen, philosophers, historians, writers, orators, and poets during the first century before Christ, the pronunciation of Julius and Augustus Cæsar, of Mæcenas, of Cicero, Virgil, and Horace, that is, the court and literary as distinct from the popular and rustic pronunciation.[1]

a Plea for the restoration of the True System of Latin Pronunciation, New York, 1859, pp. 114 ; —Dr. L. Tafel and Prof. R. L. Tafel's Latin Pronunciation and the Latin Alphabet, 1860, pp. 172, based on Corssen ; and —G. K. Bartholomew's Grammar of the Latin Language, Cincinnati, 1873, who adheres closely to the ancient grammarians.

[1] Compare Cicero's multitūdō in (N, 2—4), that is lines 2 to 4 of example N in the appendix to this tract. Ultra-Roman pronunciation of course is not to be regarded here, although of considerable philological interest. The names of Roman writers which are anglicised, as Virgil, Horace, Ovid, receive their English sounds, and in accordance with them, we must when speaking English,

ART. 6.—I assume that this Augustan pronunciation, as it may be briefly termed, differed at least as much from that of the preceding century (or pre-Augustan) as the English pronunciation of Queen Anne did from that of Queen Elizabeth ; and that it differed from that of the second and third centuries afterwards (post-Augustan and transitional) at least as much as, probably much more than, Queen Anne's from Queen Victoria's.[1]

talk of Cicero as *Sis'ser-oh*, and *Cæsar* as *Seize-her*, &c. just as we necessarily use Rome, Naples, Venice, and Florence as English words, and even without changing the spelling, give completely English sounds to Calais, Paris, Versailles, &c. It is only in recently introduced names of foreign countries, towns, and people, that those who know the languages venture to introduce the native pronunciation in English sentences. We must adopt the same course with regard to Latin names and Latin words and phrases introduced into English sentences, as we now adopt for French. But just as we should not venture to introduce the English Paris, &c. into a French sentence, so should we never think of reading one of the superscriptions of Cicero's letters, as if written in English letters *Sis'ser-oh Seize-her-eye* (Cicerŏ Cæsarī).

[1] It will be convenient to remember the following dates in reference to Latin pronunciation.

Pre-Augustan: Plautus, B.C. 254—184, Ennius (a Calabrian Greek) B.C. 239—169, Cato Censorinus, B.C. 234—149, Terence (an African freedman), B.C. 195—159, C. Gracchus (the younger tribune, see R, 3), B.C. 154—122, Lucilius, B.C. 148 - 103.

Augustan: Cicero, B.C. 106—43, Julius Cæsar, B.C. 100—44, Lucretius, B.C. 95—52, Catullus, B.C. 87—47, Sallust, B.C. 86—34, Virgil, B.C. 70—20, Horace, B.C. 65—8, AUGUSTUS, B.C. 63—A.D. 14, (Phædrus. dates uncertain, was his freedman), Livy, B.C. 59—A.D. 17, Tibullus, B.C. 54—18, Propertius, B.C. 51—? Ovid, B.C. 43—A.D. 18.

Post-Augustan: Pliny senior, A.D. 23—79, Silius Italicus, A.D. 25—100, Lucan, A.D. 39—65, Quintilian, A.D. 40—118, Tacitus, A.D. 60?—118? Statius, A.D. 61—96, Pliny junior, A.D. 61—105? Juvenal and Suetonius (close of first century ?)

Transitional, second and third century : Aulus Gellius, A.D. 117—180, Terentianus Maurus.

Late, fourth, fifth, and sixth century: Macrobius, Servius, Priscian (grammarians).

It is thus seen that the Augustan period comprehends the most esteemed Latin authors. To Cicero the pre-Augustan writers were antiquated. To Quintilian the Augustan writers were antiquated. A difference so apparent in the style of writing would naturally be accompanied by a difference of pronunciation. Cicero and Horace are our only real authorities for Augustan speech. Even inscriptions are not sufficiently safe. Quintilian is the next best. Terentianus,

ART. 7.—I assume that this Augustan pronunciation differed in almost every characteristic point from the Victorian pronunciation of English, and therefore also of Latin, and that Englishmen will consequently have to pay close attention and take much trouble to obtain an approximate conception of its nature, in theory and practice.[1]

ART. 8.—I assume also that we are not in a position to obtain more than a very rough conception of its details,[2] but even the small results that we can reach are useful in helping us on the road, and are of special pedagogical value as well as of linguistic interest.

ART. 9 —I assume that so far as the mere pronunciation of the isolated letters are concerned, the syllabus set forth by Professors Palmer and Munro, would give a result nearly as intelligible to Cicero, as an Italian's, or German's, or Frenchman's attempt to pronounce English, when only taught by books which gave keywords in their own languages, would be to an Englishman ; that is,

Maurus, and Aulus Gellius are to be regarded with suspicion, and the late grammarians knew nothing of the older pronunciation but by a tradition which they could not realise.

[1] Classical teachers seem to have hitherto acted upon Dogberry's principle that "to write and read comes by nature," (*Much Ado*, 3, 3, 16). French and German masters have to bestow much time upon mere reading. Are not Latin and Greek also foreign languages to Englishmen?

[2] I cannot too strongly insist upon this point. Even after months spent in Paris with French in the air all round, very few Englishmen are able to obtain more than a rough conception and indifferent execution of a pronunciation so utterly different from their own. Latin was at least as different, and yet we have to grub it up from passing remarks made by writers two thousand years old to others who, owing to their own habits of speech, knew what they meant by a mere allusion, and to piece these remarks together into some sort of a practical and practicable whole. The wonder is, not that our results are rough, but that they are complete enough to be usable.

not quite so good as a Scotsman's English in a Londoner's ears, but still an infinite advance on the current
English pronunciation of Latin, for that would have un-
doubtedly been mere gibberish in the ears of Augustan
Romans.

ART. 10.—Being obliged to assume some kind of a
pronunciation, I shall therefore give the vowels *a, e, i, o,
u,* their sounds as heard in London in *father, there,
machine, bore, rule,* but keep them pure when they become short, exactly as in modern Spanish, and never
allow the long sounds of *e, o* to become diphthongal by
the appendage of an *i* and *u* sound, as in English *say, so,*
often called *sēi, sōu.* The diphthongal forms *ae, oe,* I shall
render by a broader *e,* like the German *ä* in *sprächе.*
The diphthong *eu* will be like that heard for *ow* in Kent,
and often in London, all*ow* me n*ow;* beginning with *e* in
there, while *au* will begin with *a* in *father,* as in German
haus; both end with *u* in *rule.* And *ui* will be much
like *ooi* in *cooing,* but monosyllabic.[1] The letters *i, u,*
when forming a consonant, I shall treat as English *y,* and
German *w.* The latter is produced by sounding *v*
without allowing the lower lip to touch the upper teeth.[2]

[1] The relative *qui = qu + i* has become *chi* (pronounced *ki*) in Italian, but *cui*
= *c-ui,* or *qu-uī,* ancient QVOEI, has remained *cui* (nearly *cū-i*) in Italian. Did
Quintilian distinguish the sounds (1, 7, 27)?

[2] Using *v'* for this German sound, *w, v* for the English sounds, and *ŭ* for the
pure Latin vowel *u* run on as a diphthong to the next vowel, any one who wishes
to arrive at a conclusion respecting the Latin consonantal *v,* must learn to
pronounce and distinguish readily, the four series of sounds : ŭa ŭe ŭi ŭo, wa we
wi wo wu, v'a v'e v'i v'o v'u, va ve vi vo vu. These sounds were pronounced to
the audience when the paper was read on which this tract is founded. Observe
that *ŭu* was impossible as Quintilian observes, who assumes the Eolic digamma
as the sound: in hīs *seruus* et *uulgus* Aeolicum digammon dēsīderātur (1,
4, 8); nostrī praeceptōrēs *seruum ceruumque* U et O litterīs scripsērunt, quia
subiecta sibi vōcālis in ūnum sonum coalescere et confundī nequīret ; nunc U
geminā scrībuntur eā ratiōne quam reddidī ; neutrō sānē modō vōx, quam sentī-

The letters *c*, *g* will always have their so-called "hard" sounds in *sceptic, get*.[1] *H* initial will be taken nearly as in English, especially when sung, that is with its jerk without its hiss.[2] After a consonant as in *th, ch, ph, h* will be simply neglected. *Qu* will be treated precisely as in English, that is, as a single letter, phonetically a labialised *k*. *T, D* will also receive their English sounds,

mus, efficitur ; nec inūtiliter Claudius Aeolicam illam ad hōs ūsūs litteram adjē-cerat (1, 7, 26). My own belief is that in the oldest form of the language *i, u* were always vowels, which initially diphthongised with the following vowel as *ia, ua*, and that this stage was recognised, at least in writing, as long as *Ii, ūu*, we e replaced by *i, ūo*, but that when *Ii, ūu*, (or as we usually write, and as will here be always written, *ji, vu*) were employed, the sounds were those of German *j, w*. I have more doubt about *f* than *v*. It is probable that the real Augustan pronunciation hovered between *ūo, v'u*, but as Quintilian adopts the latter (if, as many think, the digamma which *he* knew, to say nothing about Homer's, was *v'*). I shall use it as being nearer to our old habits. I do not think English *w* was ever used In modern Italian: uomo, uovo, have *ūo* not *vvo*. The vowel character of *i, u* was perhaps never lost after a consonant. Thus in the Benares pronunciation of Sanscrit although *y, v*, initial have their regular English values, (*v* with the teeth), yet after consonants they remain the pure Latin vowels *i, u*, though still written as *y, v*, to shew that they do not form distinct syllables. Such double forms as : áb-jete abí-ete, fluv-jō'rum fluvi-ō'rum, could scarcely have arisen from other habits. They are quite similar to ; á-grī, ág-rī, hereafter considered.

1 The following well-known passage, justly insisted on by Prof. Blair, seems to have been too much overlooked in the warm controversy on this subject : it surely conclusively shews that Quintilian, at least, pronounced C with the same sound before all vowels: nam K quidem in nullīs verbīs ūtenduin putō, nisi quæ significat, etiam ut sōla pōnātur ; hōc eō nōn ōmīsī, quod quīdam eam, quotiens A sequātur, necessāriam crēdunt, cum sit C littera, quæ ad omnēs vōcāles vim suam perferat, (1, 7, 10). C of course determines G. As to S, the English z sound has only been "developed" in French and Italian, and has not yet touched Spanish. It was unknown to Greek, and though in modern times the ζ, (originally *zd* ?) has drifted into z, σ remains as s.

2 This effect is produced by bringing the vocal chords together so that they should be ready to emit the vowel sound immediately, and should not allow un-vocalised breath to precede, by not holding them too tightly together, and by driving the breath through them at first with a little impulsion of the muscles of the lungs. All this is easily imitated by opening a valve and jerking slightly the bellows of an accordion or concertina, so as to make the commencement of the note louder than what follows. Of course it is impossible on such an instrument to produce the effect of H in any other way. See (Art. 51) note.

though it scarcely admits of doubt that these were as unknown to the Latins, as they are now to most Europeans.
But these sounds are most easy to English organs, and
Englishmen sometimes reside for years on the continent
without perceiving the difference, or live years in India,
(where both sounds are used, and help to distinguish
words,) without knowing anything about it, as probably
Cicero would have known at once.[1] *S* will also be
always "hard" like *ss* in *hiss*. *R* will always be strongly
trilled; to which un-English but common Scotch
fashion, great attention must be paid. Final *M* will
be fully treated later on. The foreign *y*, I shall
generally treat as *i*, perhaps Cicero made it the
French *u*, for he seems to have been fond of a bit of
Greek (O, 9), and he may have called *z* either *dz* or
zd, but this is a mystery. Had I occasion to use it in
Latin I should say *dz*, for that is still heard in Italian,
but the letter occurs only in Greek words, where, owing
to the Greeks' apparent absence of power to say τσ and
their fondness for στ, the combination *zd* appears more
probable than *dz*.

It is not to be concluded that I consider these sounds
to be perfectly correct or even justifiable by any authorities which can be cited. On the contrary, it is probable
that many exceptions occurred, and many slight distinc-

---

[1] All Indians recognise the English T, D, as their own *cerebrals*, and the
French, Italian, and general European T, D, as their *dentals*. For the dental,
the tongue is pressed against the teeth as for the two English TH. In Cum-
berland, Yorkshire, and Derbyshire, at least, if not elsewhere in England, these
dental T, D, are heard in connection with R, as TR-, DR-, or -TER, -DER,
and are often confounded with the two TH by Southerners. The Irish version of
them seems to be slightly different. The Scotch, and midland and southern
English know nothing of them; but in the counties referred to, varieties of
speech are distinguished by their use. The subject is fully treated in my *Early
English Pronunciation*, Part IV. (in the press).

tions prevailed among Augustan literary men of which we can form no adequate conception. But these rough approximations will probably suffice for all school purposes.

ART. 11.—I assume that the Latin accent consisted solely in raising or depressing, or in first raising and then depressing the musical *pitch* of the voice at which a given syllable was uttered, and that this use of the acute, grave, and circumflex inflexions of voice respectively was quite independent of the *loudness* of tone, and (except as regards the third or circumflex accent) of the *length* of tone, although the determination of the precise syllable on which it immovably occurred in every word of more than one syllable, *did* depend on the length of that syllable or on the length of the adjacent syllables, as we shall see. The law of this relation was, however, different in Latin and in Greek, and there is nothing exactly corresponding to it in any European language. The nearest approach to the sound of the Latin accent is now found in Swedish and Norwegian, but the laws of its use are quite different. I assume, therefore, that the *relative pitch* of every syllable in every Latin word, was *fixed*, so far as higher and lower was concerned, that is, that it never varied in position in whatever part of a sentence the word was used, and that this position depended on the length of the syllables (M. 3—5).[1]

---

[1] This is the only result at which I can arrive after very careful study. The expressions of Cicero seem all to point to "acūta vōx" meaning a high pitch of voice, and "gravis vōx" a low pitch, independently of loudness. The terms "intendens, contentiŏ," from tightening strings, and "remittens, remissiŏ," from slackening springs, point the same way. The extreme confusion that prevails in the use of the words "raising and lowering the voice," as speaking either at a higher and lower pitch, or else with greater and less loudness, renders almost all that is usually said ambiguous. Thus when Mr. Roby says : "Accent is the

ART. 12.—Next, reserving the nature of length for close consideration presently, I assume that long and short syllables were invariably and carefully heard and distinguished, so that any error was instantly felt and detected,—as it would often make nonsense as : mala mâla, just as a *wick pool* would probably not be understood if said for a *weak pull*—that it was the main-stay of rhythm both in prose and verse, so that no rhythm was possible to an Augustan Roman which did not observe it, and that no rhythm was pleasant which did not make the relative positions of long and short distinct. (N.[1] O. P. generally).

elevation of the voice with which one syllable of a word is pronounced," either kind of elevation might be meant, though mere *increase of loudness* is rendered probable, not certain, by what follows, " in comparison with the *more subdued tone* with which the other syllables are pronounced," (Grammar § 296). Corssen's remarks on Latin "betonung" (ii. 794—892), are unhappily one mass of confusion from this cause. Hence I have been extremely careful in my own language. It is I find almost impossible to get any intelligible account of accentuation in any living language from any living speaker, so little has the subject been studied ; nor, although I have thought upon it much and have observed speakers often, am I yet able to come to any definite conclusion upon the nature of what is usually called *accent* even in French and English. The later Latin grammarians, such as Priscian, had no real knowledge of what was meant by quantity and pitch accent, which had become quite as obsolete and traditional in their day as in our own. For details on this subject, see my paper on "the Physical Constituents of Accent and Emphasis," Transactions of the Philological Society for 1873—74, pp. 113—164.

[1] In my paper on *Accent and Emphasis* (just referred to) I had originally read *ūna syllaba* in (N 1) as a nominative. Mr. Roby kindly pointed out to me that it is probably an *ablative*, and should be read *ūnā syllabā*. After re-reading the whole context, I entirely agree with him. Cicero in §§ 170—173, is speaking about rhythm generally, and mentions Aristotle's rule, "is igitur versum in ōrātiōne vetat esse, numerum jubet," διὸ ῥυθμὸν δεῖ ἔχειν τὸν λόγον, μέτρον δὲ μή· ποίημα γὰρ ἔσται, and after referring to Theodectes, and Theophrastus, proceeds to say : " who would put up with people that disapprove of what these authors say, unless they were ignorant that these authors had said it ? Now if this is the case, (and I think it is) because they are not influenced by their own senses, have they no feeling of imperfection, of want of finish, of mutilation, of lameness, of redundancy? Why [here the extract in N begins] the whole audience in a theatre would cry out if a verse were shortened or lengthened by a single

ART. 13.—I assume, however, that rhythm did not depend solely on the length of syllables, though the laws of versification have apparently no other basis, but that the position of the pitch accent or highest pitch of the voice, in a word, was also operative, and that it was to secure variety here that the laws of cæsūra in Latin verse were gradually developed.

ART. 14.—Lastly I assume that the Augustan Romans had *no* force accent, that is, that they did not, as we do, distinguish one syllable in every word *invariably* by pronouncing it with greater force, that is, with greater loudness than the others, but that the force varied according to the feeling of the moment, or the beat[1] of the

syllable. And yet the common people know nothing of feet, nor observe any rhythm, nor have any idea what offends them, nor why, or in what particular it offends them. But nature herself has put into our ears the power to appreciate (jūdicium) all long and short quantities in sounds, and rising or falling inflections in speech." This is the only consistent interpretation which I can put on the last sentence, and this fully bears out what I have said in the text.

[1] Barred music (quite a recent invention, arising from the discovery of polyphony, or the power of singing several melodies by different voices at once without creating confusion, a thing unknown to the ancients) depends upon exactly equal intervals of time regulated by the beat of the conductor's bâton or foot, and it is a rule that the note played to the *first* beat in a bar, should be slightly louder than that on the third, and this again louder than that on the second (in both triple and common time), which should itself again be generally slightly louder than that on the fourth (in common time). But this comparative loudness which forms the undercurrent of rhythm and helps to "mark the time," though very conspicuous in dance music and marches, is constantly overruled by the laws of *forte* and *piano*, *staccato* and *legato*, just as the precision of the length of the intervals is overruled by the directions *accelerando* and *lentando*. Now there may have been such an *ictus* in Roman verse, but it was often not at regular intervals as we shall see (Art. 105) and it certainly never overruled, (as in our music also it never overrules) the musical pitch and length, or even the emphatic loudness of individual notes. Let the English reader then who knows music, remember that *ictus* can only apply to the conductor's beats or the interval between two of them ; that such intervals were not necessarily of the same length (owing to introduced *lentando's*): that *quantity* answers to the time of duration of any note (as crotchet or quaver) ; and *accent*, in Latin, to the alterations of pitch by ascending or descending the musical scale, this being

timekeeper in singing, and was used for purposes of expression ; just as with us, musical pitch is free, that is, just as we may pronounce the same word with different musical pitches for its different syllables, and in fact are obliged to vary the musical pitch in interrogations and in replies. The fixity of musical pitch and freedom of degrees of force in Latin, and the freedom of musical pitch and fixity of degrees of force in English, sharply distinguish the two pronunciations even irrespective of quantity.

II. Elementary Exercises on Quantity.

ART. 15.—Having by these assumptions cleared the way for work, I shall endeavour to develop the feeling for Latin quantity or syllabic length, and Latin accent or comparative pitch by suggesting a graduated series of exercises which shall lead up finally to reading Latin in its own rhythm, with due regard to sense. I shall not actually give all the exercises at length but rather hint at the pædagogical process than carry it out, as any teacher will be immediately able to do so for himself. But as an additional assistance I shall state the intention of each step, which of course must remain a secret to the pupil. The

determined by the number and length of the syllables of the word sung (just as if when several were combined in one word, and the last but one was a quaver, the others being semi-quavers, the quaver should have the highest pitch) ; while *force* answers to the *forte* and *piano.* Hence all four, *ictus* (or beat), *quantity* (or length), *accent* (or pitch) and *force* (or loudness) are naturally independent of each other, although habitually they may be made dependent one on another, or several of them upon something else (as a musical or intellectual conception). Latin accent consists in fixing the syllable of a word which should have the *highest pitch* ; English accent consists in fixing the syllable of a word which should have the *greatest force.*

case presumed is that which is at present most common,
where a school teacher who wishes to instruct his higher
class of pupils that can already translate Latin with
tolerable ease, but have hitherto used the English barbaric pronunciation, or, having accepted the new method,
have not sufficiently realized the action of varied length
and varied musical pitch, upon the values of the letters.
When the pupil is altogether ignorant of Latin, the case
is slightly different, and perhaps easier, for he has no bad
habits to unlearn, and will be considered hereafter.

ART. 16.—*To develop the feeling for division of time.*
Use a pendulum swinging about four times in a second.[1]
Class say la ! la ! &c. once to each swing in chorus, then
la ! lala ! la! lala ! one la ! for the first, and two for the
second swing.   Then la-a ! la ! la ! la-a ! la ! la ! keeping
the la-a ! two swings, and so on.   Try the same exercise
with all the vowels in succession (sounds as in Art 10, of
course), and without any consonant.   Shorten string of
pendulum to about 3 inches and try again.[2]

ART. 17.—Take the vowels in any line of Virgil
and pronounce the short (one swing) and long (two swings)
without consonants ; thus A, 2 gives *e i o e ū e e o ō i i
a ā ā*, where the line over the vowel signs indicates a long
vowel.   Repeat the exercise without pendulum.   Make

---

[1] Take a yard of sewing thread and tie the ends ; pass it through and over the
loop of a common key. This makes a pendulum which answers every purpose.
By shortening the string when held between the fingers, any degree of rapidity
can be obtained ; between 9 and 10 inches of length gives quarter seconds.

[2] More complicated divisions of time, as in music, are not needed. The method
of giving instruction in that case has been well developed from a French model
by the Tonic Solfaists, see : The Standard Course of Lessons, and Exercises in
the Tonic Sol-fa method of teaching music by John Curwen, edition of 1872, pp.
160, see pp. 7, 8, 18—20, &c. under *taa-tai-ing.*

the class feel at least an appreciable difference of length. Continually increase speed.

To shew the slight effect of an *initial* consonant, try the same exercises with different initials *p, b, t, d, c, g, f, s, r, l, m, n, j, v, h.* Take care in saying *pe, pi, po, pe, pū,* to run the consonant on to the *following* vowel, and *avoid* running the vowel on to the following consonant.

ART. 18.—*The nature of syllabication has now to be developed.* This consists in the running of a consonant on to a vowel, by a *glide,* and of the vowel by another glide on to the following consonant. Both glides may be indicated by proximity of the letters. In saying *pe pi,* guard against *pē pī* (long vowels,) *pepi* (second vowel long, second *p* gliding on to both vowels), *pepi* (both vowels short, glide as before). Develop the feeling of each as distinct from the other. In *pepi* observe that even less time is lost between *pe* and *pi* than in *pe pi.*

ART. 19.—*To develop feelings of pitch and force as independent of length.* Represent raised pitch by an acute accent ('), increased force by a turned period (·) ; lowered pitch and diminished force are not specially represented. The reader is particularly requested not to confound the acute accent (mark of raised pitch) with the turned period (mark of increased force), and to remember that they are totally distinct (Art. 14). In the well-known song *non più andrai* farfallo*ne amoro*so,* the loudest and longest notes are given to the syllables preceding the *, but each of these is lower in pitch than the preceding syllable. Distinguish *pe pi* (uniform length, pitch, and force), *pé pí, pe pí,* (both, uniform force), *pe· pi, pé pí·, pe· pi. pe pí·,* (all with short vowels, and without

running the vowels on to the consonants). Vary as *pé i,*
pe i, é pi, e pi, pé i, é-pi, &c. Then distinguish *pépi,*
pe·pi, pē·pi, pē·pi, and so on, where *p* glides on to both
vowels. Vary with all the consonants. This exercise
requires great practice to obtain ease and certainty of
execution. Write on blackboard and make whole class
follow.[1] The final rising pitch does not occur when
both syllables belong to the same word in Latin, but it
constantly occurs when the syllables are distributed
between two words.

ART. 20.—*To develop the effects of "position."* First
take doubled consonants. Distinguish accurately between *pépi* (as in pepper), and *péppi* (as in dee*p p*ool).
The form *pépi* is not Latin but English, *peppi* is rare in
English, except in compounds or between words and
frequent in Latin, even within the same words. Compare English *pity, city, silly* (only one *l* heard), and pu*t t*o
it, se*t t*o, the grea*t t*oe is grea*t*er, we *l*ie, (one *l*), we'*ll l*ie
(two *l*s), ti*ll* eight (one *l*), ti*ll l*ate (two *l*s), pe*nkn*ife (two
*n*s), pe*nn*y (one *n*). Thou slee*p*est, thou slee*p-p*est! Mi*ss*y
mi*s-s*ent:—u*nkn*own and u*n*owned ! Latin a*n-n*us, to*l-l*it,
es·se te*r-r*a. The effect is the same as that of doubled
consonants in Italian. It is difficult for an English organ
to acquire when not occurring in compound words. The
doubled *r* as in *terra* is particularly difficult for English
speakers, and should be well practised. No relaxation
of the organs, no puff of wind or grunt of voice should
intervene between the two parts of a doubled consonant,

[1] The following direction is of the utmost importance. "The teacher never
sings [speaks] *with* his pupils, but sings [utters, reads, dictates] to them a brief
and soft *pattern*. The first art of the pupil is to *listen well* to the pattern, and
then to imitate it exactly. He that listens best, sings [speaks] best." Curwen's
Standard Course, p. 3. See also (Art. 96).

which should more resemble separated parts of one arti-
culation than two separate articulations.[1]

ART. 21.—Next take two consonants not forming an
initial combination. The Latins had not the power we
have of combining many consonants. Final consonants
were always well developed, and there was sensible rather
than perceptible pause[2] before beginning a new syllable
with a second consonant. Make this clear by a hyphen
in writing, as is uniformly done in the Appendix. Try
imaginary words as *pép-si· pep-sí·* (varying force and
pitch). Initial Latin combinations consisted of *p, b, t,*
d, c, g, followed by either *r* or *l* (*tl, dl* are not used in
Latin, and *dr* is rare) and sometimes *n* and *s* or preceded
by *s,* or rarely both. In all these cases the vowel might
(within the word) be always run on to the first consonant,
as *pép-ri,* or not run on as *pé-pri.*[3]

III. The Artificial Rhythmical Unit of Latin Speech.

ART. 22.—The preceding studies are on natural quantitative rhythm, the following are on the form they have
assumed in Latin itself. A Latin syllable is to be considered to end in its vowel when this is possible, and is
then called open. The length of time occupied by the
preceding consonants is disregarded, even when there are

---

[1] Duplication of consonants is consequently regarded simply as the energetic
utterance of a single consonant, as will be subsequently explained. It plays a
great part in all quantitative languages as Sanscrit, Persian, Arabic.

[2] That is, one rather felt by the speaker than the hearer, not quite amounting to
Quintilian's unbecoming pause (Art. 85).

[3] Of course the vowel might be either long or short in this case, as *pḗp-ĭ ē.*
But the former usage seems confined to poetry (Art. 24) and the latter is doubtful.

two or three as *stā-*, *scrī-*.   The syllable ending in a vowel is considered to be long or short according as the *vowel* it contains is long or short, and as this length is not marked in Latin books, a knowledge of it has to be acquired for each individual word.   This is a task absurdly difficult for learners, and all Latin books now printed, whether for school or other purposes, and not merely dictionaries and graduses, *ought* to have the vowels which specialists (often with great difficulty) have ascertained to be *long*, properly distinguished by the sign of length.   When the schoolboy makes a mistake here, it is the *editor*, not the boy, that should be punished. The editor *ought* to have known, and the boy trusted the editor.   But all of us, big or little, are foreigners (Art. 7), and have no knowledge of the word but what its letters give us, and hence we should be always properly treated by editors.   The orthography used in printed Latin books is notoriously not that of their writers. Hence there is no objection to this little improvement.[1]

---

[1] Quintilian as a Roman knowing words by ear, finds that it is below a grammarian's dignity to determine what letters should be used in a word except in cases of doubt: rectē scrībendī scientiam—cūjus ars nōn in hōc posita est, ut nōverimus quibus quæque syllaba litterīs constet (nam id quidem infrā grammaticī officium est) sed tōtam, ut mea fert opīniō, subtīlitātem in dubiīs habet (1, 7, 1).   Hence he finds it supremely foolish to put the long mark on all long syllables, but admits that it is necessary to know an appletree (mālus) from a bad man (malus), a post (pālus) from a marsh (palūs), [by the bye, if the reading is correct, (it can be easily altered,) Horace says *palus*, with both short, in : rēgis opus; sterilisque diū *palus*, aptaque rēmīs, A. P. 65, where of course he might have written : sterilisque palūs quondam, or even : sterilisque palūs diū, with a long vowel shortened in hiatus, as in Cicero's, Q, 13] and nominatives from ablatives : ut longīs syllabīs omnibus oppōnere apicem ineptissimum est, quia plūrimæ nātūrā ipsā verbī quod scrībitur patent : sīc interim necessārium, cum eadem littera alium atque alium intellectum, prōut correpta vel prōducta est. facit, ut *mālus* arborem significet an hominem nōn bonum, apice distinguitur · *palus* aliud priōre syllabā longā [pālus] aliud sequentī [palūs] significat ; et cum eadem littera nōminātīvō cāsū brevis, ablātīvō longa est, utrum sequāmur. plerumque hāc notā, monendī sumus (1, 7, 2—3).   For foreigners who have

ART. 23.—When on account of two or more consonants following which cannot begin a word, the syllable is bound to terminate in one or more of them, then, whether the *vowel* is long or short, the *syllable* is considered long. This occasions great difficulty in determining whether the vowel *is* naturally long or short.[1] As a mere matter of convenience, having no Augustan ears to discover the error, or Augustan sense to determine what is right, and guided by many other considerations, I shall usually treat such vowels as short.

ART. 24.—Even when the consonants are capable of beginning a syllable as in *a-grō*, the vowel is sometimes run on to the consonant, and the first syllable made long as *ag-rō*, (see ag-ricolam, D, 9) but we may readily suppose that this occurred only in poetry.[2]

not heard and used the word over and over again till it is ingrained, but who have to gather it by the eye from time to time, sometimes once in a year, the ambiguity which Quintilian even as a Roman felt for sense, remains in all cases for pronunciation. "Position" is determinable by easy rules, and hence, except to warn beginners (as in the Appendix), need not be marked. But the *naturally* long vowel *should* be invariably marked, as it is throughout this tract.

[1] There is an old bad custom of putting a long mark over the vowel in a syllable which is long by "position," as : āgrēstem. We must distinguish between the long vowel and the long syllable. Of this word *agrestem*, Quintilian says, *a* brevis, *gres* brevis, faciet tamen longam priōrem [syllabam], (9, 4, 86). Cicero says : *inclitus* dīcimus brevī prīmā litterā, *īnsānus* prōductā, *inhūmānus* brevī, *īnfēlīx* longā, et, nē multīs, quibus in verbīs eae prīmae litterae sunt, quae in *sapiente* atque *fēlīce*, prōductē dīcitur ; in cēterīs omnibus, breviter : itemque *composuit, cōnsuēvit, concrepuit, cōnfēcit :* cōnsule vēritātem, reprehendet : refer ad aurēs, probābunt : quaere, cūr? ita se dīcent juvārī : voluptātī autem aurium mōrigerārī dēbet ōrātiō (*Or.* § 159). This shews clearly that the length of the *vowel* did not depend upon " position," as the bad notation alluded to, seems to imply.

[2] Quintilian says : ēvenit, ut metrī quōque condiciō mūtet accentum, ut *pecudēs pictaeque volúc-rēs;* nam *volúc-rēs* mediā acūtā legam, quia etsi natūrā brevis, tamen positiōne longa est, nē faciat iambum quem nōn recipit versus hērōus (1, 5, 28). This shews that he would naturally say *vólucrēs* as an anapest, and that *volúc-rēs* was merely poetical. Similarly : quæ fīunt spatiō, sīve cum

C

ART. 25.—When the vowel was short the consonant was necessarily dwelt upon, and even a slight, and when the consonant was mute, quite perceptible pause, was probably made between the consonants as in *ac-tūs* (Art. 21).

ART. 26.—In words ending with a consonant there was always a possibility of a following consonant to lengthen the last syllable, and even when the word ended with a vowel there might follow a troublesome initial combination, creating position. Hence perhaps it arose that the length of a final syllable having a short vowel was unsettled, and a short syllable might be used for a long one. At the end of a clause, a syllable, no doubt, was often lengthened, and Cicero repeatedly tells us that length was indifferent in such cases (P. 1—3).

ART. 27.—Syllables ending in a short vowel, not run on to the following consonant, were taken as short. Even where it seems that the vowel must be run on to the consonant, if a following vowel allows the separation of the consonant from the preceding vowel, I think, that this medial consonant was probably attached in speech to the *following* only and not to the preceding vowel as well. This was almost certainly the case in the middle of a word, and was probably the case at the end thus *mē-di-u-ses-t = medius est.*[1] The words were run on

syllaba correpta prōdūcitur, ut *Italiam fātō profugus*, seu longa corripitur, ut *ūnius ob noxam et furiās*, [*ūnius* for *ūnīus*] extrā carmen nōn dēprehendās ; sed nec in carmine vitia dūcenda sunt (1, 5, 18).

[1] Mr. Roby (Grammar, p. 87, §§ 272, 273, and preface, p. lxxxiii., 2nd edition, adopts the English habit, as in *critical,* where the first syllable ends with the glide of the first *i* on to *t,* and the second begins with the glide of *t* on to the second *i.* Notwithstanding the reasons he has adduced in the passages cited, I incline to think that the Latins did not speak thus. So far as I can judge, modern Italians do not. When a consonant occurred between two vowels as in

in all cases very closely together, without any gaps.   In fact, as Cicero says, Latins were not allowed to divide their words (Q. 8).   This is the practice in almost all languages.   We complain of French use in that respect,

famēs, there was, I think *no* glide of the first vowel on to the consonant, as of *a* on to *m*, but only of the consonant *m* on to *ē*.   The glide from vowel to consonant occurred only when at least two consonants followed, and was even then not compulsory if these two consonants could form an initial combination.   In other words no such glide occurred without "forming position."   At the end of a clause this was always assumable.   In position then the vowel glided on to the first consonant, and then if the consonant was mute, silence ensued ; if not mute, the consonant itself sounded a very short time.   The second consonant glided only on to the following vowel.   If we use the minus sign (−) to shew absence of glide, and the plus sign (+) to shew presence of glide, it seems to me that Latin famēs = f + á − m + ē + s, annus = á + n − n + u + s, agrō = á − g + r + ō, erunt = é − r + u + n + t ; whereas English famine = f + a + m + i + n.   The question is exceedingly difficult.   Frenchmen as a rule assert that their own medial consonant belongs to the second vowel only.   The late Mons. A. C. G. Jobert, who spoke English admirably, and was a man of science as well as a teacher of languages, could only hear the glide on to the *first* consonant (Colloquial French or the Philosophy of the Pronunciation of the French Language, 1854, pp. 191).   I had long conversations with him, but could not get him to feel that he *also* glided the consonant on to the following vowel, as I heard him distinctly pronounce.   M. Tourier (Model-book, 1851) had also noticed the glide from the preceding vowel to the consonant, but not so fully.   M. Favarger, a living French teacher, who has carefully studied pronunciation, after for a long while refusing to recognise the first glide on to the consonant, in a recent conversation with me stated that further observation constrains him to admit it.   These facts serve to shew the great difficulties in the way of the investigation even in living speech, and to explain the hesitation with which I speak respecting Latin, especially when it is impossible to enter into the numerous little reasons which collectively make me incline to the opinion here expressed.   This opinion may be made the ground-work of a practical pronunciation, but when the vowel is thus separated from the consonant Englishmen will be apt to lengthen it, and this is certainly a worse error than running it on to the consonant ; fā′ − mae and fá − mē must be kept quite distinct.   The pitch accent must be carefully separated from the force accent, and then much of the difficulty will be overcome.   If however fá + m + ē is said, care must be taken not to fall into fá + m − m + ē as in flammae, which perhaps an Augustan Roman would hear in the English sound ; that is, hearing a new sound he would refer it naturally to that most familiar to his own organs.   At least such is the habit of all moderns.   These remarks apply especially to the pronunciation of both *cane* and *Cannae* like the Scotch *canny*, and so on in other words, as *virī* like English *virile*, *homo* like English *hommage*, *tremor* like English *tremour* or *tremble*, &c. which I believe to be mere English expedients to keep the vowel short, but might have served to lengthen the syllable to a Roman's ears.

C 2

the French complain just as much of English use.   It
is only the foreigner who breaks up a sentence into un-
connected words.

ART. 28.—Now the most artificial part of the Latin
and Greek quantitative rhythm, consisted in taking
a short vowel, or syllable as the unit of length, and
supposing that it was always of the same length, and
that the long vowel or syllable was of exactly twice
that length.   Nothing of this kind is likely to have
occurred in speech or declamation, but may have occurred in chanting, and must have occurred in simul-
taneous chanting.   Cicero found Greek lyrics entirely
wanting in rhythm when the music was absent, and
had great difficulty in following some of the comic
metres when the piper was not present to mark the
time (O. 9—14).   Hence the artificiality is apparent.
Still to begin with, this artificiality must be aimed at,
because we have nothing like it in English except in
barred music, with crotchets and quavers (Art. 14,
note).   In English singing the consonants are reduced
to nonentities, and the short vowels lengthened on
long notes.   Later Greek and Latin chanters *did* play
such mad pranks occasionally, (p. 28, note) but the
older rhythms were very much simpler, the music was
merely to steady the voice, and it was important that
the words should be intelligible.   That they read
the verse in a semi-chant, if not a full chant, is scarcely
to be doubted.   That even declaimers did so sometimes, the story of Gracchus's piper told by Cicero leads
us to think (R. 2—7).   But from what Cicero himself says, I think that *he* did not chant much more than
many of our own public speakers, especially when they

indulge in *orotund*[1] delivery. Even declaiming without a vestige of chant, is not a century old in English, and many English readers always chant poetry, or read in a peculiar style totally different from their prose habits, just as their prose reading differs from their ordinary speech. In English, however, the inflexion of the voice is free, except in the final cadence. In Latin it was fixed for every word.

ART. 29.—To make all long syllables of the same length or nearly so we shall have to take liberties with the lengths of their vowels and consonants. The rhythmical relations are, however, best studied in combined syllables called *feet*. In all the following examinations of length, set your pendulum to the length of time which you wish your short syllable to occupy, and reckon *one* single swing for a *short*, and *two* single swings (or one double swing) for a long syllable. Instead of a pendulum, the teacher may use rapid finger taps, if he can trust himself for making them sufficiently isochronous. Then the fall of the finger, or the rise is a *short* length, and the rise and fall together a long length. For some feet, spondee, dactyle, anapest, choriamb, this answers well ; but difficulties arise for trochees, iambs, pæons,

---

[1] Adopting the favourite elocutionist's adjective made from *ōre rotundō*, compare Quintilian: sit autem in prīmīs lectiō [of verses] virīlis et cum suāvitāte quādam gravis, et nōn quidem prōsae similis, quia et carmen est et sē poētae canere testantur: nōn tamen in canticum dissolūta nec plasmate (ut nunc ā plerīsque fit) effēminata: dē quō genere optimē C. Caesarem praetextātam adhūc accēpimus dixisse: sī cantās, male cantās; sī legis, cantās (1, 8, 2). This affected plasma was evidently something approaching to a high pitched orotundity, for he compares it to harmonics on a pipe: nec verba in faucibus patiētur [hīc magister] audīrī, nec ōris inānitāte resonāre, nec, quod minimē sermōnī pūrō conveniat, simplicem vōcis nātūram plēniōre quōdam sonō circumlinīre, quod Graecī καταπεπλασμένον dīcunt. Sīc appellātur sonus tibiārum, quae praeclusīs quibus clārescunt forāminibus, rectō modo exitū graviōrem spīritum reddunt (1, 11, 6. 7).

epitrites, &c., which will require the interval between *two* taps to be taken as the standard short, and hence involve very rapid tapping. The exact equality of division is not ultimately of much importance. Its primary use is to destroy our own modern Western habits in which quantitative rhythm is not known. When a teacher can hear a native pundit read some lines of Sanscrit, or a native Arab or Persian literary man read some Arabic or Persian poetry, where the rhythm is still entirely quantitative, and observe how grand and marked the long syllables stand out from the short ones, although the latter are not hurried over, he will have a better notion of quantitative rhythm as a reality, than he can educe by any amount of mere reading and imagining.

ART. 30.—The length of syllables may be marked by the teacher as in this tract, and in the quantitative examples. The diphthongs " ae, oe, au, eu, ui," are always long. The vowels " ā ē ī ō ū " are also always long and all other vowels are short, so that the short mark becomes unnecessary. A short vowel followed by another vowel or by a single consonant or an initial combination of consonants, ends a short syllable. A long vowel under the same circumstances ends a long syllable. Any vowel long or short or any diphthong followed by a consonant with a hyphen after it, occurs in a long syllable. After a very little practice it will be found unnecessary to mark "position," by putting this hyphen after the consonant which ends the syllable. But it should be added in exceptional cases, as, " ág-rō volúc-rēs." The invariable place of highest pitch in each word should be marked by an acute or circumflex according to rules subsequently given, (Art. 41) but of course well known to the teacher.

The variable position of force should be marked by a
turned period, or by underlining on the black board.
Pupils should be encouraged to mark the naturally long
vowel, and that only, in their books.

IV. Metrical Feet in Latin Words.

ART. 31.—There are an immense number of feet, of
which, with few exceptions, only those of two or three
syllables need be noticed.   Quintilian, differing from
Cicero, considers all others to be compound (9, 4, 79).

ART. 32.—*Pyrrhic* of two short syllables, as : mémor,
súus, méus, mála, bóna, frúor, cáne, páter, jóvis.   Here
the difficulties consist in giving the highest pitch to the
first syllable, in letting the voice fall on the second, in
not running the vowel of the first syllable on to the
following consonant, and in placing the force or loudness
sometimes on the first, and *sometimes* on the second
syllable, when the latter ends in a consonant, without
lengthening either.   This exercise requires great practice,
but it is fundamental.

ART. 33.—*Iamb*, one short and one long syllable, as :
párā, ámā, áman-t, régun-t, súōs, fórēs, plágās, déīs, chórī.
Here again the same difficulty with regard to the first
syllable occurs, and the length of the second will occasion
some trouble to pronounce it without stress.   Recollect :
"*scatter* her enemies," in *God save the Queen*, where
" scat·errr " is sung, with the first syllable very short
yet with force, and the second syllable very long and yet
without force.   In Latin, sometimes the first, sometimes
the second syllable had *force*, but the vowel was *never*
run on to the consonant, as in " scat·errr," so that *ré·gun-t*

must not fall into *rég·unt*, which might be heard as a bad *rég·gun-t*, and then would not be an iambus at all (p. 19, note).

ART. 34.—*Trochee*, or *choreus*, one long and one short syllable, as: rō'ma, vĕ'sa, mē'ta, pál-ma, rī'sus, mō'tus. This is altogether an easy foot, especially as the force need not be laid on the last syllable.

ART. 35.—*Spondee*, two long syllables, as: rē'gēs, rē'gī, vír-tūs, vén-tōs, múl-tōs, cúr-run-t. The difficulty here is to keep both syllables long, and to practise giving the force to *either* syllable without losing the length or high pitch of the other. There will be a difficulty in keeping the spondee distinct from the iambus and trochee. Decline an adjective as: mág-nus, mág-na, mág-nī, mág-nō, mág-nōs; and: cítus, cíta, citī, cítō, citōs, and mark the differences of length clearly, avoiding the common school trick of putting great force on the variable final syllable and making the preceding syllables almost inaudible, (see Art. 112). Remember that in: mág-na, mág-næ, &c. the first syllable is fully as long as the second, and that although in: cíta, citæ, the first syllable is short, it has the highest pitch and is not at all obscured or hurried over. This exercise is really very difficult to English pupils. Such English words as: turn-pike, muletrack, primrose, highway, tollbar, penknife, made to follow the phrase "we can see the —" in an *affirmative* (not interrogative) sentence, may help to give Englishmen some conception of a Latin spondee both in quantity and pitch accent.

ART. 36.—*Dactyle*, one long and two short, as: vér-tere, rúm-pere, caé-saris, ĭ'n sula. The difficulty here is to prevent the last syllable from becoming long, as in: ĭ'nsulās, forming a *cretic*, (also called *amphímacrus*) or one short between two long.

ART. 37.—*Anapest*, two short and one long, as : pópulī, mémorēs, própera. Great care has to be taken *not* to make the first syllable long, and when the force is given to the first syllable not to make it long by running the first vowel on to the following consonant, (giving a *cretic* again,) or not to do this and also not to make the last syllable short, converting the anapest into a dactyle ; or not to make all three short. Great care is necessary to distinguish pō′pulus, pópulus, pō′pulī, pópuli, mémoris, mémorēs.

Feet of Three and Four Syllables.

ART. 38.—*Molossus*, three long, as : ín-gén-tēs, in-fán-dōs, sub-mít-tun-t, and *Choriamb*, (that is *chōreus* and *iambus*), two short between two long, as : op-pósitīs, myr-mídonēs. These two feet occasion great difficulty to keep them clear and distinct. Their length is the same, but their rhythmic effect, which depends not merely on the length but on the number of syllables,[1] is very different. As these feet are often distributed among different words, the position of the highest pitch varies considerably. If the force coincides with the beat of the line, then in both molossus and choriamb, the first and last syllable have generally the stress, and in putting it there care must be taken not to make the second syllable of the molossus short. The usual bad habit is to read a molossus as one long between two short making *instantis* in position (K. 3) like *amī′ca*, which is an *amphibrach*, or one long between two short.

[1] Cicero (*Orātor* § 194) quoting from Aristotle, says : " Ephorus vērō nē spon-dēum quidem, quem fugit, intelligit esse aequālem dactylō, quem probat [Aris-totelēs], syllabīs enim mētiendōs pedēs, nōn intervallīs ēxistimat."

ART. 39.—The following examples of all the feet
which are usually spoken of by name are taken from
p. 164 of W. Ramsay's " Elementary Treatise on Latin
Prosody; (Glasgow and London, 1837, pp. 304), which
is extremely useful for the numerous examples it contains, each with an exact reference :—

DISSYLLABIC. *Pyrrhichius* casa, *Spondaeus* rēgēs, *Tro-
chaeus* Rōma, *Iambus* parens.

TRISYLLABIC. *Tribrachys* anima, *Molossus* Rōmānī,
Dactylus car-mina, *Anapaestus* populōs, *Amphibrachys*
amica, *Amphimacer* ap-pulī, *Bacchius* cantāre, *Anti-
bacchius* catōnēs (*palimbacchius* in Quintilian 9, 4, 82).

QUADRISYLLABIC. *Proceleusmaticus* habilior, *Dīspon-
daeus* Maecēnātēs, *Choriambus* Rōmulidae, *Antispastus*
Clytem-nēstra, *Dīiambus* Corinthiī, *Dītrochaeus* or *Dīcho-
raeus* (P. 1) dīmicāre, *Iōnicus ā mājōre* Lāvīnia, *Iōnicus
ā minōre* Diomēdēs, *Epitritus prīmus* venēnātis, *E. secundus* con-ditōrēs, *E. tertius* hērōicī, *E. quartus* in-
vītāmus, *Paeonius primus* Caecilius, *P. secundus* Horātius,
P. tertius Menedēmus, *P. quartus* profugien-s.

V. Elementary Notions of Verse Rhythm with both Accent and Quantity—Hexameters.

ART. 40.—After a feeling for the rhythm of these feet
has been produced, we must proceed to verse—treating
at first the so-called *elided* syllables, (of which the precise
nature is to be considered afterwards,) as absolutely non-
existent. Thus in the examples in the Appendix, wherever ‿ is used, skip the vowel before it entirely, and where
a small ᵐ is also written, skip that as well. Where a regular
final *m* is used with a hyphen after it, read it like the

next following consonant. The object is not yet to teach how to read verse, but only how to understand the action of feet in producing rhythm. Hence we reduce a verse to a mere skeleton of sound, independent of sense and of rhetorical alterations of sound. These are the muscles and nerves to be laid on afterwards.

ART. 41.—But the place of the raised pitch must be strictly observed, and for this purpose the verses had better be first read in a kind of sing-song, the high pitched syllables being all of one pitch and the low pitched syllables being all of one pitch also, but about a musical "fifth" lower than the other, as if the latter were sung to the lowest note of the fourth string of a violin, and the former were sung to the lowest note of its third string.[1]

[1] Regarding the musical nature of Greek accent, there is a most instructive passage in Dionysius of Halicarnassus, περὶ συνθέσεως ὀνομάτων, Chap. xi., which, on account of its musical technicalities, I here annex in English, giving the principal Greek expressions in parentheses. This writer, who was born between B.C. 73 and 54, and died soon after B.C. 7, lived 22 years in Rome, where he probably taught as a rhetorician. He was no doubt acquainted with the best literary men of the Augustan epoch, and though his remarks apply to Greek and not to Latin, there is no reason to doubt that the meaning of *acute, grave,* and *circumflex* accent, in Latin, coincided with ἡ ὀξεῖα, ἡ βαρεῖα, and ἡ περισπωμένη προσῳδία in Greek, of which the Latin words were mere translations. The two first words were however universally applied in Greek to raising and lowering pitch in music. The following passage serves to shew that not only the names, but the things signified were identical : " Music (μουσικη), and the science of public speaking (ἡ τῶν πολιτικῶν λόγων ἐπιστήμη), differed from that used in songs and on instruments (τῆς ἐν ᾠδαῖς καὶ ὀργάνοις) in quantity (τῷ ποσῷ), not in quality (τῷ ποιῷ). For in the latter [public speaking] words (λέξεις) have also melody (μέλος), rhythm (ῥυθμὸν), modulation (μεταβολὴν) and propriety (πρέπον). In speaking, then, also, the ear is delighted with the melody, is impelled by the rhythm, welcomes the modulations, and especially longs for propriety (ποθεῖ δ᾽ ἐπὶ πάντων τὸ οἰκεῖον). The difference is merely one of degree (κατὰ τὸ μᾶλλον καὶ ἧττον). The melody of speech, then, (διαλέκτου μέλος), is measured by a single musical interval (ἐνὶ διαστήματι) which is as nearly as possible (ὡς ἔγγιστα), that called a Fifth (τῷ λεγομένῳ διὰ πέντε). It does not rise in pitch (ἐπιτείνεται ἐπὶ τὸ ὀξὺ) beyond three Tones and a half (πέρα τῶν τριῶν τόνων καὶ ἡμιτονίου, which is the measure of a Fifth in the musical scale as from C to G), nor is it depressed in pitch (ἀνίεται ἐπὶ τὸ βαρὺ) more than this amount (τοῦ χωρίου πλεῖον). But the whole

The place of raised pitch is *not* marked, except in the first example A, but may be easily found from the

of a word (ἅπασα ἡ λέξις), considered as made up of parts (ἡ καθ᾽ ἓν μόριον λόγου ταττομένη), is not spoken (λέγεται) at the same pitch (τῆς αὐτῆς τάσεως), but one part in an acute pitch (ὀξείας), one in a grave pitch (βαρείας), and another in both pitches (ἀμφοῖν, of course, successively). Those words of one syllable which have both pitches, have a low pitch imperceptibly blended with the high (συνεφθαρμένον ἔχουσι τῷ ὀξεῖ τὸ βαρύ, the word implies a mixture by the dying off of one into the other; the low is probably placed first because it was the longer and final effect which grew, as it were, out of the high), and these we call "circumflexed" (περισπωμένας). But those words which have pitch upon different syllables separately (ἐν ἑτέρῳ τε καὶ ἑτέρῳ χωρὶς) keep its proper nature (τὴν οἰκείαν φύσιν) for each. In dissyllables there is nothing intermediate between high pitch and low pitch (οὐδὲν τὸ διὰ μέσον χωρίον βαρύτητος καὶ ὀξύτητος). But in polysyllabic words, of all kinds, there is but one syllable which has the high pitch among many which have the low pitch (ἡ τὸν ὀξὺν τόνον ἔχουσα μία ἐν πολλαῖς βαρείαις ἔνεστιν). On the other hand, the music of song and of instruments uses a greater number of intervals (διαστήμασι πλείοσιν), and not only the Fifth, but beginning with the Octave (ἀπὸ τοῦ διὰ πασῶν ἀρξαμένη), it performs (μελῳδεῖ) the Fifth, the Fourth (τὸ διὰ τεσσάρων), the whole Tone (τὸ διάτονον) and the Semitone (τὸ ἡμιτόνιον), and as some think, even the Quartertone audibly (τὴν δίεσιν αἰσθητῶς, the *diesis* was originally the same as a semitone, whence the modern French *dièse* for *sharp*, but the word was afterwards used for the later enharmonic division of the semitone, so that the interval B to C had an inserted transitional sound, which we may write δB, thus giving B— δB — C, where the lengths of the string sounding the notes were in the proportion 32 - 31—30; the English Quartertone is a very loose term, but it is generally used in this case; see the Greek Scale explained in Smith's Classical Dictionary, and more fully in Helmholtz's *Tonempfindungen*, Chap. xiv., of which my English Translation is in the press). But this [vocal and instrumental] music does not hesitate (ἀξιοῖ) to subordinate words to the air (τὰς λέξεις τοῖς μέλεσιν ὑποτάττειν), instead of the air to the words, [as in the present day, but let us hope that this did not happen till the degenerate period of Greek music in which Dionysius lived]. This is especially evident, among many others, in the airs of Euripides, which he has made Electra sing when speaking to the chorus in his "Orestes" [v. 140—3].

σῖγα, σῖγα, λευκὸν ἴχνος ἀρβύλης
τιθεῖτε, μὴ κτυπεῖτε—
ἀποπρόβατ᾽ ἐκεῖσ᾽ ἀπόπροθι κοίτας.

[The lines are here printed from the text of Tauchnitz's stereotyped edition of Dion. Hal., and this, it will be seen, was clearly his reading. But Dindorf's text runs thus:

σῖγα, σῖγα. λεπτὸν ἴχνος ἀρβύλης
τίθετε, μὴ ψοφεῖτε, μή ᾽στω κτύπος.
ἀποπρὸ βᾶτ᾽ ἐκεῖσ᾽ ἀποπρό μοι κοίτας.

These are the first lines of lyric poetry in the tragedy. It is not to be supposed that the music here criticised is that used when the play was first performed B. C. 408, that is, more than three centuries before these remarks were written, when Greek music had probably different rules]. In these lines the words σῖγα σῖγα quantity. It is *never* on the last syllable, except of course when the word has been artificially shortened for these exercises by omitting the vowel before ⏑. If the last syllable but one is long, it is spoken with a raised pitch, which is maintained throughout if its vowel is short, as : vén-tūs, vén-tōs, or if the last syllable is long, as : fā'mae ; but sinks immediately, if its own *vowel* is long, and at the same time the vowel of the last syllable short, as : fâma, to be distinguished from : fā'mā. When the word *que* is added on, the preceding syllable even if short has a raised pitch (not greater force) and this in the Appendix is marked in all the examples, as : mētáque, because it is constantly forgotten by English readers.[1]

λευκὸν are set (μελῳδεῖται) to a single note (ἐφ' ἑνὸς φθόγγου) although each of the three words has both high and low pitches (βαρείας τε τάσεις ἔχει καὶ ὀξείας, observe that τάσεις is here used for προσῳδίας). And the word ἀρβύλης, has the third syllable of the same pitch as the second (ἐπὶ μέσῃ συλλαβῇ τὴν τρίτην ὁμό-τονον ἔχει), though it is impossible (ἀμηχάνου ὄντος) that one word (ἐν ὄνομα) should have two high pitches. In the word τιθεῖτε although the first syllable is made lower (βαρυτέρα), the two that follow have both the same high pitch (ὀξύτονοί τε καὶ ὁμόφωνοι). The circumflex (ὁ περισπασμὸς) has vanished (ἠφάνισται) from κτυπεῖτε, for the two [last?] syllables are spoken at the same pitch (μιᾷ τάσει). And ἀποπρόβατ' does not receive the acute accent belonging to its middle syllable (τὴν τῆς μέσης συλλαβῆς προσῳδίαν ὀξεῖαν, where observe the use of the word προσῳδίαν *accent* as synonymous with τάσις, *pitch*, or degree of *tightening* of the string), but the pitch of the third (ἡ τάσις τῆς τρίτης, here again τάσις is used for προσῳδία), has descended (καταβέβηκεν) to the fourth syllable. Rhythms are treated in the same manner. For prose neither forces nor interchanges the lengths of any noun or verb (ἡ μὲν γὰρ πεζὴ λέξις οὐδενὸς οὔτ' ὀνόματος, οὔτε ῥήματος βιάζεται τοὺς χρόνους, οὐδὲ μετατίθησιν), but preserves long and short syllables as it has received them by nature (ἀλλ' οἵας παρείληφε τῇ φύσει τὰς συλλαβὰς τάς τε μακρὰς καὶ τὰς βραχείας, τοιαύτας φυλάττει). Yet rhythmical and musical art change them, shortening and lengthening (μειοῦσαι καὶ αὔξουσαι), till they are often reversed (ὥστε πολλάκις εἰς τἀναντία μεταχωρεῖν), for they do not rectify the times by the syllables, but the syllables by the times (οὐ γὰρ ταῖς συλλαβαῖς ἀπευθύνουσι τοὺς χρόνους, ἀλλὰ τοῖς χρόνοις τὰς συλλαβὰς)." The great value and importance of this passage, which is seldom referred to, its explicit identification of Greek accent with pitch, and its clear assertion of the strict observance of quantity in prose, have induced me to give it at length.

[1] Mr. Roby says (Gram. 2nd ed. p. lxxxlii.): "I confess to entertaining some doubts as to a short syllable, when followed by an enclitic, receiving the accent,

In other cases if the last syllable but *one* is short, whatever be the length of the adjacent syllables, the last

e.g. prĭmáque.   As the Romans would not have accented *prĭmaque* on the
penult, if it had been one word, I do not see why the *ĭ* should have lost the
accent by the addition of the enclitic." But shifting the place of the accent was
to be expected in order to shew that *prĭmaque* is *not* one word, and probably
prĭ͞maque might have puzzled a Roman at first, just as some of our English
accents puzzle the French (and conversely). Prof. Key (Tr. Ph. Soc. 1873—4,
p. 50, note) says : " I have ventured to place an accent on the first syllable of
vī͞taque, [in the last line of the *Aeneid*] rather than on the second, because I
utterly reject the doctrine of the grammarians, who contend for *vītáque,* and who
seem in this respect to have obtained the consent of Mr. Munro, see his words :
The enclitics *que, ue, ne,* attract the accent to the syllable (word?) immediately
preceding, whether long or short, *armáque* as well as *armī͞sque.* Thus in p. 389
he gives us Lavīnáque, Tiberīnáque ; and in p. 390, templáque mentis." Now
no one disputes the shifting of accent in *ármis armī͞sque,* because the last is regarded as a single word, and then the law of accent would require the shifting of
accent as in *vólucres volúc-rēs,* (p. 17, note,) and as is quite common in ordinary
inflections, as *Cícero Cicerŏnis Cicerŏ͞nī.*   On the modern force accent principle
the thing is not impossible, for it occurs in modern music but rarely, and then
only to produce a peculiar effect, as when in six-eight time the stress is laid on
the second and fifth notes.   On the other hand, on the theory of pitch, the shifting
of the accent on to a short syllable (which is equivalent to making the middle note
of a triplet the highest), is very common indeed, and may be found constantly in
the Duet *All' idea* in the *Barbiere,* thus the 10th and 11th bars have the lowest,
or a descending note in the middle of the triplets, while the 12th bar has three
examples of the highest note in the middle of a triplet, as (in the bass), using *s*
for sharp: e a g*s*, a c′ b, c′ e′ d′*s*, e′ c′ a, g.   I presume that, as in English we
naturally glide the vowel on to the following consonant when we give it force,
Prof. Key and Mr. Roby said : mētac·we, vītac·we, to the utter destruction of
any remnant of metre left by putting force accents for pitch accents in the other
words, and that both (as I have personally heard in the case of Prof. Key),
regulated the rhythm to their ear by force accents, instead of quantities.   The
result of so doing showed itself clearly in the third century, even in Italy, see
Art. 113 ; it had nothing to do with Augustan Latin.   There is absolutely no
difficulty to English organs in saying : mē·táque, vī·táque, and it is a good exercise to repeat such a combination many times in succession, beginning slowly, and
increasing speed gradually.   Observe also that Latin prepositions, &c. added on
to following words (as in Quintilian's circumlĭ͞tora in the next note), did *not*
change the position of the accent, because they were not proclitics, but *did* form
a single word with the following, whereas the shifting of the accent for enclitics
pointed out the double character of the word.   Observe also that the law of
accent in case of enclitics applies to Greek as well as Latin, and that in Greek it
even allowed two syllables with raised pitch in one word, as σώματά τε, or σῶμά τε
This was not possible in Latin, where omniáque vītáque would be said, the first
raised pitch becoming lost.   But the principle is the same, and whatever theory
is thrown out must apply to both cases.   The theory that accent consisted simply

syllable but *two* has the raised pitch which is maintained
throughout, as : īnsula, īnsulās, rúm-pere, lĭ′mite, lĭ′mitēs,
sólidā. Monosyllables have a raised pitch, as : túnc, árs,
which, if the vowel is long, falls immediately, before the
vowel is concluded, as : hî. But prepositions, relatives,
and some unimportant vocables, as *et*, *aut*, &c., acted
apparently as if they were parts of the following word
and have no raised pitch. In (A.), the raised pitch is
marked by an acute, as : ád-sum, and the low pitch is
left unmarked, except where it occurs after the high pitch
on the same long vowel, and then the circumflex accent
marks both length and change of pitch, as : ôra. Some
doubt attaches to the absolute generality of these rules.
But they are the only rules sanctioned by any persons
who were accustomed to hear the Latin we wish to
imitate, and consequently it is far better to err possibly
by carrying them out strictly, than to err certainly by
adopting any conjectures of later Latin grammarians, or
the notions of merely modern critics who have never
noticed pitch accents in their lives.[1]

in altering pitch *does* so apply. In Italian when the pronouns, &c., are added on
to a verb, they do not change the place of the original force accent, as agitan·do,
agitan·domi, invia·re inviar·tele, anda·te anda·tevene, &c., although, as in the
last instance the accent is thrown back further than would be allowable on an
unincreased word. Hence Italian has no proper enclitics. I do not indeed know
of any real modern analogues. As regards merely the use of a raised pitch upon
a syllable of little force, while the preceding syllable is long and of a low pitch,
I need merely mention that this is precisely the way in which a Swede taught
me to pronounce *skŏna*, that is *skŏ·n̆d*, where *d* is a mere unemphatic inflectional
syllable as in German *schöne*, which, except in accent, the word much resembles.
Yet this is the same as vi·tá(que), Greek οὑδέ &c.

[1] The classical rule is given by Quintilian : in omnī vōce acūta intrā numerum
trium syllabārum continētur, sīve hae sunt in verbō sōlae sīve ultimae, et in hīs
aut proxima ēxtrēmae aut ab eā tertiā. Trium porrō dē quibus loquor, media
longa aut acūta aut flexa erit ; eōdem locō brevis utique gravem habēbit sonum,
ideōque positam ante sē id est ab ultimā tertiam acuet. Est autem in omnī vōce
utique acūta sed nunquam plus ūnā nec unquam ultima ideōque in dīsyllabīs prior.

ART. 42.—Begin with hexameters, because the time of each foot is there most easily measured. (A, B, C, D,) are examples of hexameters. The great difficulty to contend with, on account of our English habits, is the due expression of those long syllables which are not under the beat of the verse, supposing that beat to fall on the first syllable of the foot.

ART. 43.—First take lines having four or five spondees, as A. 24; B. 2; C. 1, 2, 10; and D. 1, 3, 4, 6, 12.

Praettereā nunquam in eādem flexa et acūta, quoniam eadem flexa et acūta, itaque neutra claudet vōcem Latīnam. Ea vērō quae sunt syllabae ūnīus, erunt acūta aut flexa, nē sit aliqua vōx sine acūtā (1, 5, 30. 31). But he had already given an exception: cum dīco *circum lītora*, tanquam ūnum ēnuntiō dissimulātā distinctiōne [that is, speaking as if there were no separation of the words], itaque tanquam in ūnā vōce ūna est acūta, quod.idem accidit in illo *Trōjae quī prīmus ab ōrīs* (1, 5, 27). This last was taken to be *Trōjae'quī* or rather Trojae·qui, with a short vowel, and great increase of force, by Prof. T. Hewett Key, when I heard him apply it. Those who know Prof. Key's views on Latin accent, as laid down in his papers: A Partial Attempt to reconcile the Laws of Latin Rhythm with those of Modern Languages (*Trans. Philolog. Soc*, 1868—9, pp 311—351), and: Accent a guiding Principle not merely in old Comic Metres, but generally in Latin Poetry, and first of Virgil's Hexameters (*Ib.* 1873—4, pp. 35—52), will see that I hold altogether different opinions. I may mention that where Prof. Key *writes* an acute accent I always heard him *read* with rather an exaggerated increase of *force*, irrespective of *pitch.* For myself I think Quintilian meant: Trōjae, see also the passage from Quintilian quoted in (p. 17,) note. With these strict inflexible rules, Quintilian thus contrasts the Greek freedom: sed accentūs quoque, cum rigōre quōdam, tum similitūdīne ipsā, minus suāvēs habēmus; quia ultima syllaba nec acūta unquam ēxcitātur [raised, excited], nec flexa circumdūcitur [waved], sed in gravem vel duās gravēs cadit semper. [This is quite opposed to the later Grammarians]. Itaque tantō est sermō Graecus Latīnō jūcundior ut nostrī poētae, quotiens dulce carmen esse voluerint, illorum id nōminibus exornent (12, 10, 33). The fact was Greek was a foreign language which Quintilian had some difficulty in learning to pronounce, and he therefore esteemed its sweetness too highly, just as the Englishman, who in the fourteenth century, wrote those dialogues in old French which M. Paul Meyer has reprinted (from Harl. MS. 3988, in the *Revue Critique* for 1870), speaks of "doulz françois, qu'est la plus bel et la plus gracious language et plus noble parler, *après latin d'escole,* qui soit ou monde," with more in that strain. As the nature of the accent had probably entirely altered before the fifth century, next to no weight is to be attached to what the later grammarians say on the subject. They were nearly as incapable of understanding the nature of pitch accents as we are. Prof. Key has justly pointed out that they always speak of the laws of accent in the *past* tense *habuit,* not *habet.* (*Tr. Ph. Soc.* 1873—4, p. 36).

Read at first with the pendulum or tap of the finger.
Place stress at first on the first syllable of each spondee
and dactyle, afterwards vary it much, and see that it does
not disturb the quantitative rhythm.

ART. 44.—Next take lines beginning with two
spondees, and hence with five long syllables, as A. 3, 6,
19 ; B. 5 ; C. 9.

ART. 45.—Then lines with a spondee followed by
dactyle, as A. 4, 10, 14, 17, 18, 20, 22 ; B. 1, 3, 6 ; C. 5,
14, 16, 18 ; D. 8.

ART. 46.—Then those which have a dactyle and
spondee, and hence begin with a choriambus, as A. 1,
9, 11, 13, 16; B. 8, 9 ; C. 11, 12, 17 ; D. 5, 9.

ART. 47.—Then those with two dactyles, as : A. 2, 5,
7, 8, 12, 22, 25 ; B. 7 ; C. 4, 6, 7, 8, 15 ; D. 2, 7, 11.

ART. 48.—Observe the difference of rhythmical effect
in each of the cases (Art. 43) to (Art. 47).   Observe the
mode in which lines differ which begin with the same
feet, owing to the different division of the words, and
hence the different positions of the raised pitch among
the quantitative feet.

ART. 49.—Observe particularly the effect of breaking
the third or fourth foot by a caesūra, by means of which
a low pitch is secured for the beginning of the third or
fourth foot.   Examples : Break of third foot A. 1, 4, 5,
8, 10, 11, 13, 14, 15, 17, 18, 19, 21, 22, 24.   Break of
fourth foot A. 2, 3, 6, 23.   Half break, not at the end
of the first long syllable of the foot but at the first short
syllable, A. 9, causing a markedly different distribution of
the pitch of the voice.   The case of A. 7, 12, 16, 20,
where the break occurs on a vowel which is omitted in
the present exercises, really belongs to this class.

D

ART. 50.—Observe the constant form of the final
cadence, almost always dactyle and spondee, with the
high pitch on the first syllable long of each. The only
exception in (A., B., C.,) is (B. 2). Observe the remarkable effect of pitch in that line. This is very rare
in Virgil's poetry, and seems always to have been introduced for a purpose. Only some 42 examples occur
in his works, but such cases are commoner in Lucretius.
Characteristic cases are—

> Tum variae illūdunt pestēs; saepe exíguus mûs.
> > *Geo.* I. 181.
> Illīc, ut perhibent, aut intempésta sílet nóx.
> > *Geo.* I. 247.
> Prīma vel auctumnī sub frīgora, quum rápidus sôl.
> > *Geo.* II. 321.
> Ipse ruit, dentēsque Sabellicus exácuit sûs.
> > *Geo.* III. 255.
> Dat latus, insequitur cumulō praerúptus áquae móns.
> > *Aen.* I. 105.
> Vertitur intereā coelum et rúit ōcéanō nóx.
> > *Aen.* II. 249.
> Stérnitur exanimúsque trémens prōcúmbit húmī bôs.
> > *Aen.* V. 481.

There can hardly be better illustrations of the
effect of pitch accent in Latin verse. The ordinary
method of reading produces hideously unrhythmical
results.

ART. 51.—The following are Virgilian examples of
a different cadence :

> Câra déūm sóbolēs mágnī Jóvis incrēméntum
> > *Ec.* IV. 49.
> Aut lē'vēs ócreās léntō dúcunt argéntō.
> > *Aen.* VII. 634.

And the two are united in :

Cum- pátribus populôque, penā'tibus et mágnīs dîs.

Aen. VIII. 679.

ART. 52.—Having thus attuned the ears of pupils to quantitative rhythm as modified by variable pitch, we can approach the consideration of the real treatment of final vowels followed by other vowels, and of the final *m* before vowels and consonants.

VI. Slurred Vowels.

ART. 53.—Take the case of a vowel ending one word and a vowel beginning the next, when the two vowels are rhythmically reckoned together as one syllable. With this case consider that where the second word begins with H., because this H. never made position, and had probably no hissing effect, so that it readily died out.[1]

---

[1] The *chommoda hinsidiās*, and *hīōniōs* for *commoda insidiās* and *īōniōs*, mentioned in Catullus (lxxxii. or lxxxiv.) may have had a fully hissed *h*, because they were mere defects of utterance arising from an explosive manner with which we are very familiar in English, especially from uneducated speakers who try to do their bitter best (et tunc *mirificē* spērābat sē esse *locūtum*, Quum, *quantum poterat*, dīxerat *h*insidiās), and of course Catullus had no means of expressing the two varieties. In fact only one *h* occurs in writing, and phonologists are driven to great straits to express the many varieties with which they are now acquainted. (See my paper in the *Academy* for 17 January 1874, on a Physica Theory of Aspiration). The words of Cicero and Quintilian, and the slurring of vowels, which would be disturbed by the interposition of vocalised breath, lead me to consider that the Augustan Latin *h* was merely a forcible, jerked utterance of the following vowel, without any unvocalised breath, exactly as now in India for the combinations *bha, dha. gha*, &c., produced in the way explained on p. 6 n. 2, Cicero says : quin ego ipse, cum scīrem ita mājōres locūtōs esse, ut nusquam nisi in vōcālī adspīrātiōne ūterentur loquēbar sīc, ut *pulcrōs celēgōs triumpōs Kartāginem*, dīcerem : aliquandō, idque sērō, convīciō aurium, cum ēxtorta mihi vēritās esset, ūsum loquendī populō concessī, scientiam mihi reservāvī. *Orcīviōs* tamen et *matōnēs, ōtōnēs, Caepiōnes, sepulcra, corōnās, lacrymās* dīcimus, quia per aurium jūdicium semper licet (Cic. *Or.* § 160). Quintilian writes :

Cicero (see Q.) objects strongly to open vowels, which he considered to gape (*hiāre*), or ᴕᴗ meet with a shock (*concursus, conjungere*).   Yet in his writings there are constant cases of open vowels; thus in (Q.) itself: legendō oculus (1), nē ēxtrēmōrum (2), sī inconditīs (5), nēmō ut (7), illae ipsae horridulae (10), quī ut (11), saepe hiābant (11).   It is evident, therefore, that these cases were to him quite different from: scīpio invicte (12), and etēsiae in (13), where the open vowel made a distinct syllable, and that it must have been this habit of allowing open vowels to form a distinct syllable which he found so offensive in Greek, and which he declared that Roman ears could not endure if frequently repeated (Q. 6, 13), and it must have been this separation which he contemplated when he said that no Roman was allowed to pull his words asunder (dīstrahere vōcēs, Q. 9).   To Cicero therefore two vowels thus situated formed one syllable in prose, as in verse.   There is not even a hint that the first vowel was dropped.   Whenever this occurred in Greek the vowel was not written, a habit followed by

illa vērō nōnnisi aure ēxiguntur, quae fīunt per sonōs : quanquam per aspīrā-tiōnem, sīve adjicitur vitiōsē sīve dētrahitur, apud nos potest quaerī an in scriptō sit vitium ; sī H litterae st, nōn nota. [" If H is a letter," i.e. represents a separate sound, and "not a mark," i.e. represents an initial modification of sound ; this is I believe the real distinction meant by those many orthographers who since Quintilian's time have disputed whether H is or is not a *letter*].   Cūjus quidem ratiō mutāta cum temporibus est saepius.   Parcissimē eā veterēs ūsī etiam in vōcālibus, cum *oedōs ircōsque* dīcēbant, diū dēinde servātum, nē consonantibus aspīrārent, ut in *Graecīs* et in *triumpīs*, ērūpit brevī tempore nimius ūsus, ut *chorōnae, chentūriōnēs, praechōnes,* adhūc quibusdam inscriptiōnibus maneant, quā dē rē Catullī nōbile epigramma est [just cited].   Inde dūrat ad nōs usque *vehementer* et *comprehendere* et *mihi*, nam *mehe* quoque pro *me* apud antīquōs tragoediārum praecipuē scriptōrēs in veteribus librīs invēnimus (1. 5, 19—21).   It is evident that Quintilian's *h* was very small indeed, the precursor of its French, Italian, and Spanish evanescence, where it is really merely a diacritical sign, or, as we shall find Quintilian says of *m*, merely, inter duās vōcāles velut nota est, nē ipsae coeant (9, 4, 40).

modern writers generally in Italian, German, and English.[1]
French, however, does not cut out the mute vowel except
in monosyllables, because of a general rule of pronunciation. In French verse, except in very few cases, no
open vowels at the end of words, not even open nasalised
vowels are permitted. In the middle of a word, however, open vowels occur in French, making two syllables, and this was also the case in Latin; compare:
conticu-ēre (A. 1), aenē-as (A. 2), ēru-erint (A. 5), fu-ī
(A. 6), incipi-am (A. 13), e-a (A. 17), pri-amī (A. 22),
stati-ō (A. 23), abi-isse peti-isse (A. 25), and frequently.
But: svādent (A. 9), abjete (A. 16), were exceptions,
which I have indicated by using consonantal forms *j*, *v*,
without being certain that the true consonants were
spoken. There was no necessity therefore for a Latin
tongue to connect concurrent vowels into one syllable,
but it habitually did so when the two vowels belonged
to different words. It was a habit, not a necessity of
speech, but a habit on which versification reposed.

ART. 54.—Now in Spanish and Italian, the two
Romance languages most like the Latin, we find the same
ability to separate vowels internally, and the same habit
of connecting them between words. In (S.), containing
the two first stanzas of Tasso's *Jerusalemme*, 28 instances
of vowels thus connected (marked by ‿) occur in 16
lines. In (S. 3): senno‿, e, this connection occurs with a
pause after the first vowel, and in (S. 5): s'oppose‿, e‿in-
vano, not only is there a pause after the first vowel, but

---

[1] In older English when the final *e* was still a distinct syllable before a consonant, there is reason to believe that it was entirely omitted before a following
vowel, and generally even before a following *h*, and although it was still retained in writing, as indeed it still is in most cases, it has long ceased to be
sounded in any way. This is not the case even in modern high German.

there are three vowels, e -e -i, reckoned to form one syllable.   On the other hand there are real omissions of vowel before vowel in : l(e) armi, e(i)l (1), che (i)l (2), l(o) inferno, s(i) oppose (5), d(i) asia (6), s(e) adorno (15), d(i) altri (16).   But the principal omissions are before consonants, as gran(de) sepolcro (2), popol(o) misto (6), ciel(o) gli (7).   And there are other omissions so common as to be unwritten, as, *e* for *ed, a* for *ad, col* for *collo* which again stands for *con lo.*

ART. 55.—Now it is easy to hear what Italians actually say in verse, and especially in singing, on account of our Italian operas, but it is necessary to distinguish between an Italian singer and a singer of Italian, who is frequently a foreigner, and hence of no authority for pronunciation. It will be found that such singers let all the written vowels be heard, but yet bring them on to one single musical note, which may be itself very short.   The following are cases from well-known pieces of music, (technically called "numbers") in the *Nozze di Figaro.* The hyphen is used to shew the vowels forming one syllable in two words, and the superior figures shew the relative lengths of the syllables as indicated by the music, and as invariably observed by the native singers.

ART. 56.—*Nozze di Figaro*, No. 2, se-a^1 ca^{2}so^1, che^1 vuol^2 mi-il^1 pa^{1}dro^{1}ne^1, se-u^{1}dir^4 bra^{3}mi-il^1 res^{2}to^2, di^{1}scac^2-cia-i^1 sos^{1}pet^{2}ti^1.   But with the pause between two lines of verse : se-il^1 mat^{1}ti^{2}no^1 il^2 ca^{2}ro^1, il^1 ca^{2}ro^1 il^1 ca^{2}ro^1.

No. 3, very quick time . l'ar^{2}te-a^{1}do^{1}pran^{2}do^2.

No. 4, quick : è-un^3 pia^{1}cer^2 ser^{2}ba^{3}to-ai^1 sag^{1}gi^1.

No. 7, quick, to shew the effect of the pause : (separated) tos^{3}to-an^{1}da^{2}te^2—e^3 scac^{3}cia^{2}te^2—il^2 se^{3}dut^1 tor^2 ; (connected) tos^{6}to-an^{2}da^4 te-e^3 scac^{1}cia^{3}te-il^1 se^{3}dut^{1}tor^2.

No. 9, non³ più-an¹drai⁴ far³fal¹lo⁴ ne-a³mo¹ ro⁴so⁴.

No. 12, ve²ni³te-in¹gi³noc¹chia¹te¹vi².

ART 57.—This practice seems to have preserved classical traditions better than the medieval Latin hymns, which allow open vowels to form syllables, and know no quantity, as in the following prayer of St. Bernhard (H. A. Daniel's *Thesaurus Hymnologicus*, vol. iv. p. 228, Leipzig 1855), where the * marks open vowels, the (·) the louder syllables.   For-the pronunciation see (Art. 114).

> Dilata·re* aperi·re
> Tan·quam ro·sa fra·grans mi·re
> Cor·di me·o te conjun·ge
> Un·gue* il·lud et compun·ge
>   Qui* a·mat te·, quid pa·titur?
> Vi·va cor·dis vo·ce cla·mo,
> Dul·ce cor, te nam·que* a·mo
> Ad te* o·ret, ad te plo·ret.
> Te* ado·ret, te* hono·ret.

And so on.   All of this, if it could be read by an Augustan Roman according to his own habits, would sound horrible to him, and shew a most monstrous ignorance of versification.

ART. 58.— *The practical rules* hence deduced for Latin, are as follows :

a. When a vowel ends one word, and a vowel, (preceded or not by H;) begins the next, pronounce *both* vowels, quite distinctly and audibly.

b. When there is no pause between the words, run on the vowels closely together, and make the time occupied by the two sets of vowels in the one syllable no, longer than is required by the laws of the verse. The length of both will therefore have to be altered.

Thus syllabise (B. 8) hae²-tiⁱ-bieⁱ-runᵛ-tar²-tēs²-pā²-cis²-queim²- pō²-neⁱ-reⁱ- mō²-rē², soˆthat *bie* has only half the length of *queim*. Similarly: Pal²las² tēhōc² vul²-neⁱreⁱ, Pal²las², Aᴇɴ. xii. 948.

c. When there is a pause between the two words, the conjunction of the two vowels, and the accuracy of the time, becomes (like the Italian syllable) rather a matter of "faith" or practised acknowledgment, than of real audition, but generally one of the two syllables should be unduly shortened to indicate the effect. Thus (A. 25) nōs² aⁱbiⁱis²seⁱ raⁱ(tī, et)² ven²to², &c., *tī*, may be 1½ and *et* only ½; or *tī* being nearly fully 2, *et* will be nearly evanescent, (D. 8) mō²men² (to aut)² ciⁱtaⁱ mors², the *tō* and *aut* may each be only 1. But in all cases the effect of long and short vowels and diphthongs would be indicated by a practised speaker, and was no doubt felt by the poet.

As this practice is similar to the *slurring* of notes in music, I call it by the same name. See also (Art. 61).

Aʀᴛ. 59.—It is evident that when two words are closely united by slurring their final and initial vowels, they might be difficult to separate by the ear. The mode in which words are connected in all languages causes a difficulty of the same kind to foreigners, which no native feels when he hears them spoken, because he would feel any other way of pronouncing them in a phrase so "unnatural," that is unusual, that he might fail to catch the sense (p. 19). In modern writing it is customary to assist the eye by separating the words without indicating the mode of connection. In Sanscrit however the mode of connection is always written, and the native commentators have laid down rules for discover-

ing the separate from the connected furm. In some languages as English and French, the position of the greatest
force varies under different forms of combination, and
hence great difficulties arise to foreigners when they hear
the languages spoken, which entirely vanish when they
see them written.

ART. 60.—In Latin, however, the strict laws of the
position of the highest pitch must have clearly separated
the words, however closely they were run together. Every
word (with the exceptions already noted) had one syllable
spoken in a higher pitch than the rest, and only one,
and that syllable was never the last (in polysyllables)
and never further off than the last but two (Art. 41).
Hence con-ti-cu-ê-reóm-nēs (A. 1), ré-ge-reim-pé-riō (B. 6),
pró-pi-ahầec (C. 4, where ầe marks a circumflex on a
diphthongal form, or digraph), fā'-taás-pera (C. 15) &c.
were clearly separated as two words by their two raised
pitches. Observe the combinations -reóm-, -taás- in the
first and last instances. Here the first vowel is in a low
pitch, and the second in a high one, so that we might
write -rè̀óm-, -tà̀ás-, the effect being a *wave up*, or a reversed circumflex, which is a *wave down* (hầec). In
some cases, where the word on to which the slur was
made had a low pitch, this would appear to fail; but in
reality such a word was habitually treated as part of the
next, thus : dēsértō in lī'tore (A. 24) were really felt to be
divided : dēsértō inlī'tore, that is, they were treated as
two words, not three. When slurred they became : dē-
sér-tōin-lī'-to-re.

ART. 61.—Perhaps then we may supplement the rules
in (Art. 58) by the following practical usages.

If the first of the two slurred vowels is short and also

low in pitch, make it still shorter, so that the full length of both vowels makes up only the uńslurred length of the second vowel, thus in quáè-queíp-se (A. 5), *ei* takes up the time òf one ordinary short vowel only.

If the first vowel is long, whether high or low in pitch, and the second short and low in pitch, the second vowel is most shortened and may almost entirely vanish, as dē-sér-tōin-lī'-tor-re (A. 24). But if the first vowel is low in pitch and the second high in pitch, the second vowel though short must be made long enough to bring out the effect of its higher pitch, as:

Quám lépidē léxeis compós-tae?út tesséru-laeóm-nēs,

cited from Lūcīlius by Cicero (*Or.* § 149), where *léxeis* may be read léxīs.[1] This is probably a rare case, and no example of it occurs in the Appendix below.

If both vowels are long, perhaps that of highest pitch might have had the greatest length in the slur as, sub antī'-quaī'-lice (L. 9).

ART. 62.—If Cicero is not exaggerating (Q. 8) similar usages must have been even more strictly observed in

---

[1] Of course it is not easy to say what were the sounds of pre-Augustan *ei, oi, ai, uo, ou,* and I do not enter upon the question here. But Quintilian seems to have considered *ei* to be a mere digraph for *ī*, and the passage is noteworthy because it also seems to shew that he pronounced the Greek ει as *ī* also. Sēmi-vōcalēs gemināre diū nōn fuit ūsitātissimī mōris, atque ē contrāriō usque ad Accium [born B C. 170, and lived to a great age, so that Cicero as a young man conversed with him, if the words of *Cic. Br.* § 107, are to be taken in this sense], et ultrā porrectās syllabās geminīs, ut dixī [referring to 1. 4, 10, see (Art. 88) note], vōcālibus scripsērunt. Diūtius dūrāvit, ut EI jungendīs eādem ratiōne quā Graecī ει ūterentur; ea cāsibus numerīsque discreta est, ut Lucīlius prae-cipit: *Jam puerei vēnēre, E postrēmum facito atque I. Ut puerī plūrēs fiant;* ac dēinceps Idem: *Mendācī /ūrīque addēs E, cum dare fūrei Jūsseris.* Quod quidem cum supervacuum est, quia I tam longae quam brevis nātūram habet, tum incommodum aliquandō. Nam in iīs, quae proxima ab ultimā litteram E habēbunt et I longā terminābantur, illam ratiōnem sequentēs ūtēmur E geminā, quālia sunt haec *aureī, argenteī* et similia (1. 7, 14—16). We shall therefore be as right as Quintilian (though he may have been wrong), if we pronounce Latin *ei* and Greek ει as *ī*.

prose. Of course exceptions occurred in actual usage, but in our present state of ignorance we cannot do better than strictly carry out an intelligible rule which most probably held in the great variety of cases.

ART. 63.—The next step is therefore to read the examples in the Appendix in the same sing-song manner as before, with the same strict regard to quantity, but in place of leaving out the vowels preceding ◡, slurring them on to the following vowels, paying great attention to the alteration of pitch. The little ᵐ between two vowels must be entirely neglected, the vowels being slurred as if it did not exist, but the m- final must at present be pronounced as the following consonant. The proper treatment of this last case forms the next step.

VII. Treatment of Final M.

ART. 64.—The two facts to be accounted for are, that in all Augustan verse (and consequently in all literary Latin verse of a later period, because it is a mere imitation of the Augustan):—

a. Final *m*, did not prevent the preceding vowel of its own word, and the following vowel of the next, from being reckoned as one syllable, precisely as would have been the case if no *m* had intervened.

b. Final *m*, followed by a word beginning with a consonant, invariably "made position," that is, made the syllable which it terminated long.

Both cases might occur to the same word, even when a monosyllable, and in the same line, as to *dum* in

Jam satis est ! *dum* aes ēxigitur *dum* mūla ligātur.

HOR. *Sat.* I. 5, 13.

ART. 65.—The conclusion is inevitable that *m* had a different effect in the two positions, and that if the letter *m* were preserved in writing for both cases it was simply from etymological reasons, to assist the eye, the alteration of sound proceeding by a rule known to all Augustan Romans,—though a matter of difficult inquiry 2000 years afterwards. We have several similar instances in Quintilian (i. 7,) such as *obtinuit* written for *opinuit* said, and *inmūnis* for *immunis*.[1] It is quite clear from inscriptions that a revision of orthography took place at the Augustan period, and was continued in later periods. We know that *cum* in particular was *quum* as a conjunction, and *cum* as a preposition, and *ad* was the preposition, *at* the con-junction.[2] With regard to the alteration of *cum, in* in composition, some orthographical varieties occur, but that in all cases the final *m, n* was accommodated to the following letter there is no doubt, as : compōnō, cōnficiō, corrumpō, collūdō, condūcō, coeō, cohaero.[3]

ART. 66.—The same custom of writing the final consonant in the same way, in order that the *eye* might recognize the word, although in speech various combinations changed its sound and the *ear* always readily

---

[1] Quaerī solet, in scrībendō praepositiōnes, sonum quem junctae efficiunt, an quem sēparātae, observāre conveniat [this precisely applies to all other junctūrae], ut, cum dīco *obtinuit*, secundam enim *b* litteram ratiō [knowledge of verbal derivation], poscit, aurēs magis audiunt *p;* et *immūnis*, illud enim quod vēritās ēxigit, sequentis syllabae sonō victum *m* gemina commūtātur. *Quint.* i. 7, 7. We see then that "ratiō" was allowed to lord it orthographically over "aurēs" even in Quintilian's time.

[2] Iʼla quoque servāta est ā multīs differentia, ut *ad,* cum esset praepositiō, *d* litteram, cum autem conjunctiō, *t* acciperet : itemque *cum,* sī tempus significāret per *q,* sī comitem per *c* ac duās sequentēs scrīberētur (*Quint.* i. 7, 5).

[3] Prof. Blair (*op. cit.* p. 95), refers to "Lachmann on Lucretius, p. 136, touching the forms *coopertus, cocoleretur, coicere coventionid, conubium, comovisse, cognomen* &c."

recognized it under its various forms,[1] is common to many languages. Thus in French the final consonant is generally written though almost invariably omitted in speech before a consonant; compare *un peti(t) cheval*, with *un petit âne*, which is precisely contrary to the apparent Latin usage with regard to *m*. In other French words, as *a* for Latin *habet*, the final consonant is so usually lost that it is not written unless when accidentally pronounced, so that the moderns regard it as a mere euphonic introduction, as *il en a, en a-t-il?*

ART. 67.—There is a singular usage in Dutch where before a word beginning with *b* and *d*, any unvoiced letter as *p, k, f, s*, is voiced, thus zee*p*bak, o*p*doen, strij*k*bout, stie*f*broeder, mi*s*daal are written, but the italic *p, k, f, s*, are pronounced as English *b, g, v, z*, nearly as zēb·bak, ob·dūn, streig·bout, stiv·brū·der, miz·dād in Latin letters, and singularly enough this is the only case in which the sound of English *g* can occur in Dutch. On the contrary *v, z, g*, become *f, s, ch* (guttural) after all preceding consonants except *r*: thus in voe*d*vrouw, stie*f*zoon, a*f*grund, the Italic letters are to be pronounced, as *tf, fs, fch* (*ch* guttural) respectively, as vūt·frou stīf·sōn

---

[1] Writing can express but a small part of speech, leaving much to be supplied by the reader's habits. The tone of voice, the rising and falling of pitch and loudness, the pauses of speech, and so on, which form so many little commentaries upon the meaning of the words, are yet so difficult to indicate, that writing has seldom grappled with them, except to a very small extent. Hence the speaker, who knows the concrete effect, is generally ignorant of its composition. Writing therefore seeks by various contrivances to let him know the word intended, leaving him to alter it for the occasion, as he does usually "by nature," that is, by a habit acquired in childhood and confirmed by the practice of all around him. Horace's maxim (A. P. 180),

Segnius irrītant animōs dēmissa per aurem,
Quam quae sunt oculīs subjecta fidēlibus,

which should never be separated from its context, does not apply to the case of speech and writing.

af·χrund, in Latin and Greek letters.   Dutch is a language
in which the orthography has been-revised within the last
hundred years.   Hence we must not be surprised at
a single written final form in -*m* being retained in Latin,
on a revision of orthography, for cases where "junctūra"
alone constantly altered its effect.

ART. 68.—Now in Latin the neglect of *m* between
two vowels, was not a phonetic necessity of the language.
Thus if the *m* belonged to the second word there was no
difficulty : *suāve marī* was a choriamb, not a cretic, as
suāvem arā would be.[1]   If the *m* occurred in the middle
of the word as, *maxima, amet*, there was also no slurring
of the vowels.   The loss of *m* must therefore have been
merely a habit of speech.

ART. 69.—And in this respect we may observe that
the termination -*en* so frequent in German and old
English has disappeared in South Germany, and in
literary and even most dialectal English.   The first step
was to neglect *n* simply, and then to pronounce *e*, and in
this stage we frequently find the transition still in Germany.   In old English the -*e* final thus left was neglected
before a following vowel in verse, and consequently we
have, in an older state of our own language, an exact
counterpart of the Latin neglected *m*.

[1] This fact I think conclusively disposes of Prof. Blair's suggestion. Referring
to Priscian's obscure final *m*, in such a phrase as *nunquam ego*, he says "the
final *m* is almost nothing (paene nullīus vōcis), as far as *nunquam* is concerned,
but *passes over in a weak utterance to join the* e, *of* ego *closely following*, thus :
nunqua' mego, with which we may compare English *d* in the connection *baffled
investigation*, if pronounced *baffle' dinvestigation*," (*op. cit.* p. 99). But in the
first place I never noticed any Englishman so pronounce, and should consider it
accidental if I had observed anything of the kind, and in the second, the *d* in
English *baffled* is quite distinct and may not glide on to a following vowel. Blair
founds his notion of this "sort of mumbled connection," as a "passing over" of
the *m* to the following vowel on an expression in Quintilian, " ut in eam transīre possit" (9, 4, 40), which will be considered hereafter. See (Art. 88).

ART. 70.—Quintilian, when comparing Latin and Greek sounds to the disparagement of the former and glorification of the latter, speaks of the Latins terminating so many words with the "lowing" letter *m* which was never used in Greek, where it was replaced by the "pleasant ringing" *n*.[1] But Quintilian we know from the context was exaggerating, and his "lowing" *m* was merely an *eye*-sore, while the "ringing" nature of *n* as distinct from *m*, is as we know from the difficulty felt in English printing offices to distinguish the very names of the letters *en*, *em*,[2] at the least strongly imaginative. The passage is not one on which we can rely, and is in fact opposed to other more careful *dicta* of the same author.

ART. 71.—Now the question is, how was this final *m* treated in both cases by Latin contemporary writers? We have no manuscripts in which the orthography is of the slightest antiquarian value. We are driven therefore to inscriptions, (of which the orthography was very formal,) and to the occasional references to older practices in later writers.

ART. 72.—A large number of cases in which *m* was omitted in accusative, and genitive plural, and a rather larger number of cases in which it was written, in inscriptions, have been given by Corssen (I. 267—271),

---

[1] Quid? quod pleraque nos illā quasi mūgiente litterā clūdimus *m*, quā nullum Graecē verbum cadit: at illi *n* jūcundam, et in fīne praecipuē quasi tinnientem illīus locō pōnunt, quae est apud nōs rarissima in clausulīs (12, 10, 31).

[2] When in the years 1847—9, I had a printing office of my own for the purpose of printing English phonetically (issuing among other things, the *Phonetic News*, a weekly newspaper), and had the three types for the sounds of *m, n, ng*, in *sum, sun, sung*, my compositors found it absolutely necessary for the prevention of confusion, to give them names beginning with different vowels as, *am, en, ing*. I wonder whether Quintilian would have admired the "ringing" Chinese terminal *ng*, in place of *m*, or the French and Portuguese nasality. Hardly. Greek was fashionable in Rome.

who has also collected many cases, really more valuable than formal inscriptions for determining colloquial usage, where *m* is omitted in the scribblings of the walls of Pompeii (of course not later than A.D. 79) although these form a decided minority in comparison with the number of cases in which *m* was retained (I. 272), which is not surprising, as the omission of *m* was then cacographical, although it may have been orthoepical, in the sense of representing real usage. But after the third century A.D., with which we are not specially concerned, the *m* final was very commonly omitted in all words, and the stone-cutters seem to have applied the *m* at random even to ablative cases, (I. 273-6). Corssen, however, confines himself to giving the instances without reference to the initial letter of the following word, which is most important for our inquiry.

ART. 73.—As I have not the complete collections of inscriptions at hand, I will content myself with reviewing the whole of the words written with final *m* in the twenty-seven inscriptions given in Vol. I. App. B. of Roby's Grammar, adding the following words, numbering the inscriptions, giving the approximate date, and ordinary orthography. When the inscription is in verse the position is indicated in the ordinary orthography by a hyphen as in the examples of the Appendix below. Evident abbreviations and defective words are not quoted. They are mostly pre-Augustan.

I. B.C. 270-250. dono dedrot = *in ordinary ortho-graphy* dōnō (dōnum?) dedērunt.

IV. (Date not given). uicesma parti apolones = *in ordinary orthography* vicesimam partem Apollinis.

VI. B.C. 250. oino ploirume — duonoro optumo fuise

uiro—luciom scipione filios—corsica aleriaque urbe—
aide mereto = *in ordinary orthography* ūnum- plūrimī—
bonōru^m optimum- fuisse virum- (if the next word was
virōrum as conjectured)—Lūcium- Scīpiōnem fīlius—Cor-
sica^m Aleriam-que urbem- (if the next word was pug-
nandō as conjectured)—aedem- merito.

VII. About B.C. 250. donu dede = *in ordinary orthography* dōnum dedit.

VIII. About B.C. 250. taurasia 'cisauna samnio
cepit—omne loucanam opsidesque = *in ordinary orthography* Taurāsiam- Cisaunam- Samnium- (Samniō, according to Mommsen) cēpit.

IX. B.C. 189. hastensium seruei—agrum oppidumqu
—item possidere—dum poplus = *in ordinary orthography* Hastensium servī—agrum oppidumque—item
possidēre—dum populus.

X. B.C. 186. The Bacchanal inscription, which never
omits the *m*, nor the *s* nor even the *d* of the ablative in
ad, *od*, of which this is the last appearance.

XI. About B.C. 164–154. apiceinsigne dial—in genium
quibus—gloriam maior um qua re—ingreniu Scipio—
prognat um publio = *in ordinary orthography* apice^m in-
insignem diālis—ingenium quibus— glōriam- mājōrum
—quārē—in gremium- Scīpio—prōgnātum- Publiō.

XII. Not later than B.C. 134. donu danunt = *in
ordinary orthography* dōnum dant.

XIII. About B.C. 135. magna sapientia multasque—
quom parva—saxsum quoiei—honore is—nunquam uictus
—honore queiminus = *in ordinary orthography* magnam-
sapientiam- multasque—quum parva—saxum cui—hono-
rem is—nunquam- victus—honorem- quīminus.

XIV. About B.C. 135. progeniemigenui—maiorum

E

optenuilaudem ut—creatum laꞔtentur stirpem nobili-
tauit = *in ordinary orthography* prōgeniem- genuī [a
doubtful amendment of a clearly defective original]—
mājōru^m obtinuī laude^m ut—creātum laetentur; stirpem-
nōbilitāvit.

XV. Between B.C. 146 and 134. romam redlieit—
aedem et signu herculis = *in ordinary orthography*
Rōmam rediit—aedem et signum Herculis.

XVI. Date soon after XV., down to XXVII., "at the
end of the republic," never omit *m* final, or nominative *s*,
or insert ablative *d*.

ART. 74.—It must be observed that these inscriptions
very rarely double any consonants in writing. Even the
careful Bacchanal inscription (X.) is full of words like :
dueſonai baſanalibus eſent habuiſe ueſet adeſe adieſe
iouſiſent, with single consonants = *in ordinary spelling* Bellōnae Bacchānālibus essent habuisse vellet
adesse adiise jūssissent, with double consonants.

ART. 75.—Now the rule with regard to variations from
ordinary orthography occurring in the writing of early or
unpractised writers in any language, is, that the deviations
are always on the side of pronunciation. Cacography is
always a surer guide to sound than orthography, because
it is due to Quintilian's "aurēs" and not his "ratiō."
Orthography depends upon rules which had to be laid
down because other considerations outweighed phonetic
reasons, and which are consequently ill followed by those
who do not appreciate those reasons. The historical
character of orthography, also, always makes it more
archaic than actual usage. There is no need to go beyond English and French for proofs of this. A long
study of the English usages and examination of older

works on orthography and orthoepy, leaves no doubt in my own mind on this point.[1]

ART. 76.—An examination of these inscriptions would therefore lead me to the following conclusions.

First, that final *m* had no appreciable sound at all when final, or before a following word beginning with a vowel.

Secondly, that final *m*, before a following word beginning with a consonant, had no sound of *m*, but became appreciable in speech, either by lengthening the preceding vowel, or by doubling the succeeding consonant.

Thirdly, that the phonetical omission of the ablative *d*, (the vowel preceding it being always long), was connected with the orthographical restitution of the accusative and neuter *m*, to prevent the eye from confusing ablatives and nominatives with accusatives, and did not necessarily imply any restitution of the sound of *m*.

In the second conclusion there is an alternative hypothesis of lengthening the preceding vowel or doubling the succeeding consonant, because the inscriptional orthography would have been the same in either case. The supposition that orthographers could have actually omitted the final *m* and doubled the following consonant in writing, at a time when doubling consonants under any circumstances was so rare, is not tenable.

ART. 77.—Two questions necessarily arise with regard to these conclusions. First, is there any analogue in any known language? Secondly, is there any basis for such an hypothesis in Cicero and Quintilian? We need not inquire further, for it is self-evident that these conclusions

---

[1] See numerous instances in my *Early English Pronunciation with especial reference to Shaksfere and Chaucer*, 1869—71.

would explain both the facts (*a, b*) of Augustan versification with which we started (Art. 64).

ART. 78—Now the two languages which most closely
resemble Latin are Spanish and Italian. Spanish has
lost the habit of doubling consonants altogether, but it
almost invariably omits this final *m* in the words taken
from the Latin. Italian, however, does double consonants. It also almost invariably omits the final *m* of
the Latin.[1]

ART. 79.—Italian, however, also frequently omits other
Latin finals, as *t, d*. In this case there are two treat-
ments, one orthographical and the other orthoepical,
which bear a striking analogy to the conclusions just
drawn from the inscriptions, and which, in point of time,
first led me to conceive this solution of the difficulty.

ART. 80.—First, the omitted Latin letter is never
written in Italian when it is not pronounced. Thus *ad*,
et are in Italian *a*, *e* generally, but occasionally *ad*, *ed*
when required for metre. The bare *a*, *e* are slurred, as
e invano (S. 5), *ai* = *ad i* (S. 7); but *ad*, *ed* make
syllables as :

miro· tut·te co·se, ꭒ*ed* in Sori·a.

TASSO, *Ger.* I. 8, 1.

re·co *ad* un' al·ta‿origina·ria fon·te.

Ib. I. 30, 5.

---

[1] The qualification "almost" before " invariably" is necessary because there
are a few words, chiefly monosyllabic, in which a trace of nasality remains, Latin
cum, sum, spem, are Italian *con, sono, spene*(?); Latin *quem, tam*, are Spanish
quien, tan; Latin *rem* is old Spanish *ren*, French *rien ;* and on Roman inscriptions *con, quen, tan*, occur. But *jam* has lost its *m* everywhere. The *m* of the
accusative has quite vanished, except in *mon, ton, son.* for *meum, tuum, suum.*
These and other particulars may be seen in Diez. The object here is to arrive
at general conclusions, not particular exceptions. It is impossible to attempt a
list of exceptions in Augustan speech, where even the general rules are reached
with difficulty (see Art. 8).

The employment of *ad*, *ed*, is rare and archaic, and confined almost to poetry. It is comparable perhaps to the occasional use of *m* final to preserve the preceding syllable in Lucretius,[1] if indeed the latter are not, as I believe, really cases of unslurred open vowels which occur much more frequently (Q. 11). See also p. 65.

ART. 81.—Next, in certain cases, words, in which the omitted Latin letter is not written in Italian, are connected orthographically with a following word. beginning with a consonant, and *that consonant is then doubled to the eye as well as the ear*, thus replacing the omission by assimilation. Thus *già che* = Latin *jam quod*, become *giacchè; già mai* = Latin *jam magis*, become *giammai; con lo* = Latin *cum illo*, become *col* (S. 3, and compare the preserved *con la* in the same line for the usual *colla*); *già sia ciò che* = Latin *jam sit ecce-hoc quod* become *giassiaciocchè; ciò che* = Latin *ecce-hoc quod* become generally *ciocchè; a dio* = Latin *ad deum*, become *addio; a fatto* = Latin *ad factum*, become *affatto; a fine che* = Latin *ad finem quod* become *affinchè; a lato* = Latin *ad latus* become *allato; a le arme* = Latin *ad illa arma* become *allarme*, whence our *alarum, alarm*, and *a le* is generally *alle; a mano* = Latin *ad manum* become *ammano; e bene, e poi, e pure* = Latin *et bene, et posteā, et pūrē* become *ebbene, eppoi, eppure; da vero* = Latin *de ad verum* become *davvero; o vero, o pure* = Latin *aut verum, aut pūrē*, become *ovvero oppure; sì bene, sì fatto* = Latin *sīc bene, sīc factum* become *sibbene, siffato; il dio* = Latin *ille deus* become *Iddio* the one God. Again the perfect tenses ending on -*ò*, -*ì*, when a *lo, vi*, &c. is added on,

---

[1] Nam quod | flūvidum | est ē | lēvibus | atque ro | tundīs.—II. 464.
Sed dum a | best quod a | vēmus id | ēxsupe | rāre vi | dētur.—III. 1094.

become -ollo, -ovvi, &c., as: *ei dimostrollo* [for *dimostrò lo*] *a lungo* (Tass. *Ger.* i. 29, 7);~*amovvi* for *amò voi*, and so on.

ART. 82.—Thirdly, when, as is most frequently the case, words from which a final Latin consonant has been dropped in passing into Italian, are not *written* in connection with the following consonant, they are still *spoken* in connection with it. For this observation I am indebted to Prince Louis Lucien Bonaparte. He considers the following consonant in this case to be " energetic " (Art. 20) and to preserve this character at the beginning of a phrase.[1] In the first stanza of (S) all the words preceded by a hyphen are thus energetic, according to a copy which the Prince was good enough to make for me himself, and so distinct is the phonetic effect, that when I was reading out the stanza to him, he corrected me in every case where, from want of habit, I neglected

---

[1] The following is a translation of the rules prefixed to Prince L. L. Bonaparte's Sassarese Sardinian translation of St. Matthew (1866), with the exception of two omitted at his own request. The Italian text may be seen in my *Early English Pronunciation*, p. 799 note. "Simple consonants are often pronounced like double consonants in Italian, according to the following general rules: 1. When they are initial and commence a phrase, either at the beginning of a sentence or short clause, or after a vowel: 4. When the preceding word, although ending in a vowel, has the force-accent on the last syllable, or is a monosyllable, in both cases derived from a Latin word ending in a consonant which has been suppressed in passing from Latin to Italian. Thus the preposition *a* from Latin *ad*, the conjunction *e* from *et*, and *sì* from *sīc*, *nè* from *nec*, and truncated words as *amò* from *amāvit*, *potè* from *potuit*, have all the property of making the initial consonant of the following word energetic. Hence though we *see* the written words: a Pietro, e voi, sì grande, nè questo nè quello, amò molto, potè poco ; we really *hear* nothing but: appie'tro, evvo'i, siggran'de, necques'to necquel'lo, amom'mol'to, putep'po'co. In other cases the consonant remains weak [single]. Thus in: di Maria, i doni, la mente, le donne, mi dice, ti lascia, si gode, ama molto, pote' poco, molto largo, the initial consonants are spoken as written, either because the preceding words are the Latin *dē, illī, illa, illae, mē, tē, sē, potuī*, which end in vowels, or because in the case of *a'ma mol'to, mol'to lar'go*, the words *a'ma* and *mol'to* are not accented on the last syllable."

to make the consonant "energetic."[1]   Taking only the
cases where this "energy" supplies the place of an
omitted consonant, we find practically: al·lu·i (S. 5);
ec·con (S. 3), ed·di (S. 6), es·sot·to (S. 7); liberod·di
(S. 2), oproc·col (S. 3), armod·da·sia (S. 6), dief·favo·re
(S. 7), soffrin·nel (S. 4).   Observe that two syllables have
the force accent in certain cases, distinguishing two
united words from a single word, as the Latin pitch
accent was supposed to act in Art. 60.

ART. 83.—Taking account of Cicero's emphatic de-
claration of the necessity of connecting words in Latin
speech (Q. 9), and remembering that Italian is the descendant of at least some form or forms of Latin speech,
(not necessarily or probably of the literary Augustan form,
and hence in some cases shewing usages not traceable
to that form,[2]) is it too much to suppose that an Italian
usage, exactly conformable to what we may assume as
the colloquial forms indicated by old inscriptions, was
also the old Augustan usage for final *m*?   To me it
seems that very strong and direct contemporary evidence
would be necessary to lead to any other conclusion, and
hence I proceed to examine the second question of Art. 77.

ART. 84.—What is the contemporary evidence?   It is
neither much, nor clear.   Cicero's consists simply in
stating that *cum nōbīs*, was not said, but either *cum autem
nōbīs*, or *nōbīscum*, to avoid the sound of *cun nōbīs*.[3]   To

---

[1] This happened a year before this paper was written.   This is mentioned to
shew how the hypothesis here developed originated.

[2] To these might be attributed the rare preservation of nasality as *sono* for both
sum and *sunt*, so that an original confusion of these words is possible.

[3] The reason he gives and its application, like most old pieces of linguistry,
are almost impossible to credit: quid illud? nōn olet unde sit, quod dīcitur, *cum
illīs*? *cum* autem *nōbīs* non dīcitur, sed *nōbīscum*? quia sī ita dīcerē ur, obscaenius
concurrerent litterae, ut etiam modo, nisi *autem* interposuissem, concurrissent.

this must be added Quintilian's *cun nŏtīs*, where, however, he endeavours to give a phonetic explanation of the assimilation. And this explanation requires attention, because, although valueless in itself, it seems to imply that final *m* in his time was considered so difficult to pronounce before a consonant, that it had to be either assimilated to it, (as in the Italian examples), or entirely omitted. If we may credit him, Roman organs could not pronounce[1] their final *m* purely, without making a pause after it, and before the following consonant.

ART. 85.—Quintilian's words in reference to *cum nŏtīs*, are : quia ultima priōris syllabae littera, quae ēxprimī nisi labris coeuntibus non potest, [that is, if *m* is expressed at all, the lips are closed, but so must they be for the common *b*, *p*,] aut intersistere nōs indecentissimē ["most unbecomingly," this does not refer at all to the meaning of the words, but to the unbecomingness of the hesitation] cōgit, aut continuāta cum īnsequente in nātūram

ēx eō est *mēcum* et *tēcum* : non *cum me* et *cum te*, ut esset simile illīs *vōbīscum* atq 1e *nōbīscum*, Cic. *Or.* § 154. Such as it is, however, Quintilian echoes it for *cun nōtīs hominibus*, which he therefore puts in the order *cum hominibus nōtīs*, and he gives several other instances, much more difficult to enter into, where accidental combinations of words may be twisted into dirty senses, until Quintilian is forced to exclaim: quod sī recipiās, nihil loquī tūtum est (8, 3, 44—47).

[1] Any unusual combination of even usual šounds creates a difficulty to the speaker. An Irishman, when I remarked to him on the inconsistency of the Irish pronunciations of *machine fatigue* as rhyming to English *seen plague* respectively, made the extremely just observation, that if you were to ask an Irish peasant, he would tell you it was much "*a*ísier" to speak so than to make them rhyme to either English *seen league* or *rain plague*. The case is that of habit only. Prof. Blair (*ibid*, p. 97), quotes from "Servius in II. Dōnāti ēditionem, ap. P. p. 1797 : nēmō enim dīcit *cum mē, cum tē*, propter cacophaton," which in view of *dum mē, dum tē*, is simply absurd. But Servius had always heard *mēcum tēcum*, and hence anything else sounded wrong, as in English *I goed* (really the good old *yode*) for *I went*. Italians, who usually say *me·co te·co* sometimes indulge in *con me·co, con te·co*. It's well that Servius can't hear them !

ējus corrumpitur ["broken down, assimilated," probably not implying a censure on what was an exceedingly common Latin custom]. *Quint.* 8, 3, 45. Now with regard to shutting the mouth, it must be remembered that the lips and tongue are in exactly the same position for *p*, *b*, *m ;* and that they are also in the same position (though different from the last) for *t*, *d*, *n*. Now does Quintilian mean to say that. he could not distinguish *abnuit* from *annuit* (which had absolutely contrary meanings), without an "unbecoming pause" after *ab* in *abnuit*, to prevent the *b* from being "broken down" into *n* and thus making *annuit?* He would probably have been very much surprised at the question. But his phonetic reasoning applies strictly to this case, which he never contemplated, because he was thinking only of his habits respecting final *m*, and these, as I gather from his words, were so ingrained, that he could not pronounce without considerable effort and an "unbecoming" hesitation, that "lowing" sound *m*, whose presence at the end of words he found so offensive in Latin when he wanted to depreciate his own language in respect to Greek (12, 10, 31) ; see Art. 70, note 1. Such inconsistencies are very common with persons who write on subjects they have not studied scientifically, and very few indeed have considered it at all necessary to attend to the real nature and science of speech sounds. Quintilian always speaks as if the matter were so elementary that it was beneath his notice, and consequently writes hurriedly, inconsistently and insufficiently, which is a great loss to modern investigators of ancient habits of speech.

ART. 86.—These are really all the indications which I can find of the use of *m* final before consonants in the

Augustan and post-Augustan centuries. So far as they go they confirm the conclusions from the inscriptions and from Italian usage. It is of no use referring to Priscian and Donatus, except to note that Priscian says that *m* final had an "obscure" sound,[1] because we know for certain that for at least a century before his time, final *m* could not have been pronounced at all, and hence this use of "obscure" enables us to estimate the meaning of Quintilian's "obscuration" of *m*, before a vowel, which we shall have to examine presently.

ART. 87.—Before proceeding to this observation of Quintilian, I will refer for a moment to Verrius Flaccus, his contemporary, whose work on orthography might have been of much service in this respect. The following statement is made on the authority of Velius Longus, a contemporary of Macrobius, who belongs to the late

---

[1] Prof. Blair (*op. cit.* p. 93), and Corssen (I. 263), quote Priscian (the first as I. 555, the second as I. 38, *H*, I have not verified either), thus: "M obscūrum in ēxtrēmitāte dict ōnum sonat, ut 'templum ;' apertum [as if there could be an open mouthed M !] in principiō, ut 'magnus ;' mediōcre in mediīs, ut 'umbra.'" Now all phonologists know that initial consonants have generally *less* sound than that which it is *possible* to give to final consonants, and that consonants which are followed immediately by other consonants in the same syllable or adjacent syllable, may be variously altered. In w at sense Priscian meant his *apertum* and *mediōcre*, it would have been probably very difficult to determine, even in a *vīvā vōce* examination (judging from much experience), but what he meant by "obscure" is very clear; it was simply that *m* was written and *not* sounded. "Obscure" implied no more than this. Dōnātus ad Ter. Adel. II. 1, 53 (as quoted by Prof. Blair, *ibid.* p. 93), says: *mussitāre*—dictum a *mūtō*, vel ab *m:* quae littera est nimium pressae vōcis āc pēne nullīus [really, when final, absolutely mute, in his time,—he lived in the fourth century and was the master of St. Jerome, the writer of the Vulgate,—] adeō ut sōla omnium quum inter vō-cālēs inciderit, atterātur atque subsīdat [is ground up and settles down, like grit in water?] We know that *m* is so far from being naturally "nimium pressae vōcis āc pēne nullīus," that it can actually be *sung* upon, not only in ordinary *humming*, but as a singing part in Mozart's *Flauto Magico*. Had Dōnātus any notion of "energising" the following consonant? His expressions at least do not contradict such a theory. That the practice may be common without being observed, I at least know from having lived a year in Italy without observing it.

grammarians. He says in his orthography (Blair, p. 94, Corssen I. 26; P. p. 22, 38): nōnnullī synaloephās [junctūrās of Quintilian] quoque observandās circā tālem scriptiōnem ēxistimāvērunt, sīcut Verrius Flaccus, ut ubicunque prīma vōx *m* litterā fīnīrētur, sequens ā vōcālī inciperet, M non tōta, sed pars illīus prior *N* tantum scrīberētur, ut appāreat ēxprimī nōn dēbēre. That is, Verrius Flaccus wished to shew by partial defacement that an M though written, was not pronounced, just as "mute letters" are underdotted, italicized, or printed in skeleton type, in various systems of teaching to read English. Here only the case of final *m* preceding a word commencing with a vowel is mentioned, for if a consonant followed, Verrius Flaccus would probably have considered that the *m* was pronounced, though assimilated, as the *effect* would have been different had no *m* been there at all.[1] It must be remembered, however, that we have not the precise words of Verrius Flaccus but only a report of them furnished by a writer in whose time this *m* was certainly not pronounced at all, and that probably much more existed in the original.

ART. 88.—The classical passage in reference to final *m* before a vowel is in Quintilian. He has been speaking of junctūrae, and of the disagreeable effect of the concurrence of certain letters (Q. 2, 3) which "in commissūrā

---

[1] I have myself been told that *gh* in English *sight* and *e* in English *site* were "pronounced," because if they were left out, the words would be *sit*, and have an entirely different sound! We are, I believe, indebted to Mr. B. H. Smart for a distinction, important in reference to Latin final *m*, that the italicised letters in the English words, me*a*l, charco*a*l; fli*e*s, fo*e*s, du*e*s; pa*i*n, e*i*ther, su*i*t; bro*o*ch, do*o*r; so*u*l, bo*w*l; pl*a*y, ke*y*; Messia*h*; mat*e*, bath*e*, past*e*, ag*e*, ac*e*; g*u*ess, g*u*ide, plag*u*e, &c. "are mute, though in general significant." (Pronouncing Dictionary, 1836, Art. 171). This amounts to distinguishing marks of separate sounds, from marks used diacritically to modify the other marks, that is, "litterae" from "notae," according to Quintilian, as we shall presently see.

verbōrum rixantur." He notices *ars stūdiōrum,* and the
Lucilian omission of *s* final in *Aescṛṇīnu(s) fuit, dignu(s)
locōque,* which was evidently so strange to him that he
could never have noticed it in speech, and he goes on to
say : inde *belligerāre, pōmeridiem,* et illa censōriī Catōnis
diee hanc, aequē M littera in E mollīta, [the letter M
"softened" to E, "in the same way" *aequē;* the phrase
must have meant *diem hanc,* and the double *ee* probably
stood for a long ē, and shewed that there was no elision;[1]]
quae in veteribus librīs reperta mūtāre imperītī solent,
et dum librāriōrum īnsectārī volunt īnscientiam, suam
confitentur.[2] atquī eadem illa littera, quotiens ultima
est et vōcālem verbī sequentis ita contingit, ut in eam
transīre possit, [so that it can "pass over into it," that is,
be "softened" into it, as in *diee* for *diem* just cited, and not,
"be pronounced with the second vowel instead of with
the first," see Art. 68, note ; see also the expression
dissimulātur in the passage referring to the same practice,
quoted in Art. 137], etiamsī scrībitur, tamen parum
ēxprimitur, [is "little" expressed, euphemistic for minimē
= "not at all," the word really means, "not enough,"
"not so much as it ought to be considering that it is
written,"] ut *multum ille* et *quantum erat :* adeō ut paene

---

[1] Quintilian says in the passage referred to by him in the quotation on p. 42,
note : in ipsīs vōcālibus grammaticī est vidēre—quae ut vōcālēs junguntur aut
ūnam longam faciunt, ut veterēs scripsērunt, qui geminātiōne eārum velut apice
[as a mark of length] ūtēbantur, aut duās (1, 4, 10). Hence *diee* would = *diē.*
This would allow us, in the absence of proper types, to use double vowels for the
capitals of initial long vowels, as OOrātor = ōrātor, a practice which would be
quite unambiguous. When a word is entirely in capitals, a small letter inter-
posed would mark length, as OoRAaTOR, LAaOCOOoN. In the examples of
the appendix, capitals have been entirely avoided, but in general quotations, and
in modern editions of classical works, the above antique practice, slightly varied
to prevent ambiguity, might be adopted.

[2] Editors of old texts, please to copy !

["almost," the usual orthographical saving clause], cūjusdam novae litterae sonum, [really "sound"? see what follows] reddat. neque enim ēximitur [probably merely, it is not omitted in writing, with a feeling that it could not be left out in general spelling because of its action before a consonant], sed obscūrātur ["made inaudible," compare Priscian, as quoted in Art. 86,] et tantum aliqua inter duās vōcālēs velut nota [a mark, not a sound by itself, see on *h*, Art. 53, note] est, nē ipsae coeant. Then he goes off at a tangent on the necessity of being able to divide words rightly : videndum etiam nē syllabae verbī priōris ultimae sint prīmae sequentis, [instancing most singularly cases in which no difficulty could have occurred], id nē quis praecipī mīrētur, Cicerōnī in epistolīs ēxcidit : "rēs mihi invīsae vīsae sunt, Brūte :" et in carmine : ō fortūnātam nātam mē cōnsule Rōmam. (9, 4, 39—41). Now the points here are that the *m* almost acts as another letter, (like that of Verrius Flaccus?) to which Quintilian indeed attributes a sound (sonum), although he owns almost in the same breath that it only acted as a mark of separation, like the stonecutters (.) ! Now, years ago when I read this passage, I was misled to think that the "parum ēxprimī" implied that *m* was expressed in speech "somehow," if not "enough," and to think that the "neque ēximitur" referred to its not being altogether left out in speech instead of to its not being omitted in writing, and that the "obscūrātur," and the "paene cūjusdam novae litterae sonum" referred to that nasalising of the previous vowel which is to this day expressed by a following *m* or *n* in French, and *m* in Portuguese, so that *m* is thus applied to a particular means of modifying vowel

sounds.[1]   But in the first place nasalisation is strange
to Italy, even to its dialects (with rare exceptions).
Next in French there is every reason to suppose that
nasalisation of vowels did not exist till at least a century
after the Norman Conquest, and was not complete till
the seventeenth century.[2]   Again this nasality, when it
existed, did not affect the Latin final *m*, except in such
rare cases as to have no weight, for the whole of the
case-endings in *-am, -em, -um*, had disappeared before
the nasalisation of French had commenced.   I do
not know the history of Portuguese nasalisation, but I
find independent nasalisation arising in Southern German
(where certainly it sometimes implies an omitted *n*) and
in American English, while it probably exists widely in
extra-European languages.   Also I find the German *-en*

---

[1] This suggestion of mine (Phil. Soc. Trans. 1867, supp. p. 20) having been
referred to by Mr. Roby (Gram. Pref. p. lxxxiii. l. 10) in relation to this passage
of Quintilian, I wish particularly to state that I have entirely withdrawn it.
Prof. S. S. Haldeman, from whom I differ on phonetic points with great re-
luctance, adopts the nasality unreservedly (*op. ci.* in Art. 1, p. 27), referring to
the nasal anusvâra in the Sanscrit originals of Latin final *m*, to the passages from
Priscian, and Verrius Flaccus, just quoted, and to an inscription copied by
Manutius "in which a small curved line (˘) is used (at least by him) to represent M, N, and N (*ng*)." This last mark was probably merely a cursive *m* or *n*
as in modern Portuguese and Spanish, frequently degenerating into a single
straight line, of which the mathematical sign — = *m* for *minus*, is a well-known
example, and which is of constant occurrence in all medieval (even English)
MSS. where no nasality need be suspected.   Prof. Haldeman says explicitly
(*op. ci.* Art. 105): "the Latin nasal vowels are I, E, A, O, U, as ĕnĭ^m, dĕcă^m,
tă^m, flŏvĭo^m, tŭ^m," both the nasality and long quantity are doubtful to me.
What the anusvâra was originally, I do not know ; it has become in Indian pronunciation of Sanscrit a simple English *ng* in *singing*, and its mark (a mere dot)
seems to be the affixed dot by which alone the devanâgari character for this *ng*
was distinguished from that of the cerebral *d* (which is the English *d*). This
seems to point to an early use of this sound, which certainly replaced final *m*
under certain circumstances in Sanscrit, that apparently have nothing to do with
Latin. A very early Latin final *m* pure, is not disputed.

[2] See my investigation of the subject for the sixteenth century, with M. Paul
Meyer's results for the earlier period, in my *Early English Pronunciation*,
pp. 825—828.

disappearing into -*e* on the Rhine, without nasalisation.
Also certainly the same change occurred in English itself
without even a tendency to nasalisation. I know of no
passage which even slightly supports the nasalisation
theory, except that just cited, and this (which really says
nothing of nasalisation directly), may I think be inter-
preted as above, in a manner more consonant with the
expressions of orthographers and orthoepists.

ART. 89.—The result is that (excluding compound
words) we have one undoubted case of assimilation of
final *m* to following *n* in Cicero and Quintilian ; we have
also Quintilian stating that this assimilation could not
be avoided without an unbecoming pause, shewing
evidently that his organs were not accustomed to avoid
it ; we have a recorded though archaic case (*diee*) of final
m being omitted and the preceding vowel lengthened (if
indeed "diēm" ought not to have a long vowel always,
as being of the ē declension, so that it is after all a simple
case of omitted *m*) and we have an account of final M
generally before a vowel implying that it was really not
heard at all. Hence our examination of contemporary
authority rather confirms than weakens the conclusion
drawn from the usages of pre-Augustan and post-Augustan inscriptions and of modern Italian.

ART. 90.—A little uncertainty may still prevail as to
the monosyllables in -*m*, where as we have seen (Art. 78)
an *m* or *n*, or nasality is sometimes found in romance
languages. But the following examples from Horace's
Satires (which are selected especially because although
" pede certō," so that the effect can be measured without
hesitation, they are " sermōnī propius" and thus little
likely to resort to "poetic licenses," and to have been

effective must have reproduced the speech of the day, very slightly twisted to force it into metre), will shew that monosyllables were not excepted from the law of silent *m* before a vowel, but were treated precisely like other monosyllables which had no *m*.

DUM . . du^m‿ex parvō.—HOR. *Sat.* I. 1, 52.
du^m‿aes exigitur.—I. 5, 13.
nātus du^m‿ingenuus.—I. 6, 8.
nec du^m‿omnis abacta.—II. 2, 44.

TUM . . tibi tu^m‿efficient rēs.—I. 2, 97.
tu^m‿immundō.—I. 5, 84.
tu^m‿in lecto.—II. 8, 77.

NUM . . pōcula; nu^m ēsuriens.—I. 2, 115.
nu^m‿ignōta.—I. 6, 36.

CUM . . cu^m‿uxōribus.—I. 2, 57.
nūgarī cu^m‿illō‿et discinctī.—II. 1, 73.

QUUM . quu^m‿exīret.—I. 2, 30.
quu^m‿est jussa venīre.—I. 2, 122.
quu^m‿adsectārētur.—I. 9, 6.
quu^m‿est Lūcīlius ausus.—II. 1, 63.
quu^m‿Ilionam‿edormit.—II. 3, 61.
quu^m‿immeritōs.—II. 3, 211.

SUM . . quidquid su^m‿ego quamvīs.—II. 1, 74.
quid su^m‿ego? nempe.—II. 7, 80.

NAM . . na^m‿exemplō‿est.—I. 1, 33.
na^m‿ut ferulā.—I. 3, 120.
na^m‿ut multum, nīl moror.—I. 4, 13.
na^m‿ut quisque‿insānus.—I. 6, 27.
na^m‿inquīram.—II. 3, 41.

QUAM . qua^m‿ex hōc fonticulō.—I. 1, 56.
qua^m‿ex rē dēcerpere.—I. 2, 79.
qua^m‿aut aquila‿aut serpens.—I. 3, 27.

REM . . rē^m‿imperitō‿ac sī.—II. 3, 189.
committēs rē^m‿omne^m‿et vita^m‿et
cum- corpore fama^m.—II. 7, 67.

There is however one passage, where, if the reading is correct, *num* forms a short syllable before a vowel :—

num vesceris illā
quam laudās plumā? coctō *num* adest honor īdem?—II. 27-8.

where as before, and as even in *circumago circumeo* I
should incline to read as an hiatus, coctō nu—adest, circu
—ago, circu—eo. It is possible, however, that the correct
reading is "coctō nuᵐ ‿ *et* adest honor īdem," the *et* is
wanting to the sense at least as much as to the metre.[1]

ART. 91.—The general rules for the treatment of final
m which this discussion leads to are as follows. Exceptions must be admitted, but the only safe course is to
carry out the principle strictly, for there is absolutely no
means of determining what and where the exceptions
may be.

a. Final *m*, followed by a word beginning with a vowel
in the same clause, on to which, had there been no *m*,
the preceding vowel could have been slurred by the
regular rule, is *totally inaudible and ineffective*, and the
vowels are slurred just as if no *m* had been written.

b. Final *m*, at the end of a sentence, is *totally inaudible*
and the preceding vowel, like all final vowels (P. 2) is
indifferently long or short, but had better be made long
to indicate the excision of *m*.

c. Final *m*, before a pause, however brought about, is

---

[1] Horace is talking of the extravagance of eating a peacock, and says that
people would prefer it to a common fowl, if they had the choice, because it is
dear, and rare, and with a splendid plumage, as if that had anything to do with
the matter: "do you eat the plumage that you laud? has the cooked bird *still*
the same glories?" For *adest*, we should in prose most probably have had
manet, but this would not scan, and the sense is preserved by using *et adest*.
I don't know of any authority for this conjecture, but the syllable *num* before
a vowel is I think so impossible a reading for Horace, that I cannot quote the
passage without noting that it is manifestly incorrect. Even the line amātor
ëxclūsus quī distat, *agit-* ubi sēcum, eat an nōn (Hor. Sat. ii. 3, 260), is suspicious
in lengthening *agit-* by a kind of position before *ubi*, although less so than the
archaic *num* with pure *m.* Compare also *palus* for *palūs*, (Art. 22) note, which
is also suspicious. Corrections are easy as : agit quum, agit quī.

F

totally inaudible, but if the following word commence
with a consonant the vowel before *m* may be lengthened,
and in any case the succeeding consonant must be
uttered with more force, to indicate the excision of the
m, (see Art. 82, and Art. 92).

d. Final *m* before a word commencing with any consonant but *j* or *v,* is to be rendered effective by omitting
the *m,* and pronouncing the consonant as if it were
doubled, keeping the vowel before *m* short, but running
it on to that doubled consonant,[1] and the pitch of the
voice must be raised upon as many syllables as it would
have been had the words been separately pronounced.
The final *m* before enclitics *que, ne,* &c. is to be treated
in the same way. Use *cqu* for doubled *qu,* even in
namque, dumque = *nácque, dúcque.*

e. Final *im* followed by *j* is to be pronounced as *ī,* and
final *um* followed by *v* as *ū.* No other pronunciation
could have well prevailed. It may be best to pronounce
mj as *ij,* and *mv* as *uv* in all other cases, so that the
i, u which replace *m,* form diphthongs with the preceding vowel. But as a compromise, to ride over
a difficulty which there is no authority to settle,[2] the

---

[1] It is probable that the sight of *m* will occasion many teachers to object to
this rule, and to wish *m* to be made at most *n* before *t, d, n, f, v,* and *n* adul-
terīnum (*ng* English) before *c, g, qu.* I long wished it myself. But I could not
find that this would explain Augustan habits. So I let it go. Cases like conficiō,
convīcium, belong of course to an older stage of the language. The fondness
for *n* before *f, v,* is quite local. In Scotland *Banff* is written and *Bamf* said,
which shews a precisely opposite feeling, and one more in accordance with the
positions of the organs of speech.

[2] If the *m* is neglected then *jamjam* would be equivalent to *jaja.* Now if
this is treated as in ājācem, cūjus, cjus, we should say jā'jā. But it may be
questioned whether jāijā, āijācem, cūijus, ēijus, &c. would not be more correct.
This seems at least to have been the opinion of the later grammarians (Corssen
I. 301—3), but of what value is that for Augustan Latin? It is possible indeed
that Quintilian's words imply Cicero's usage to have been the same : sciat etiam

reader may always pronounce *am, em, im, om, um* as simple *ā, ē, ī, ō, ū* before both *j* and *v*. The final *m* before enclitic *ve* is to be treated in the same way.

ART. 92.—*Mode of practice.*—Rules *a* and *b* require no new practice, as the pupil is already familiar with slurred vowels. Rule *c* requires practice in giving force to the following consonant. If that is *p, t, c* or *b, d, g*, this force is produced by making the closure of the organs tighter, so that the following sound comes out more explosively, and there is the same delay between closing the organs and opening, as if *pp, tt, cc* or *bb, dd, gg* occurred before the vowel. But if the following consonant be *f, s, j, v, m, n, l, r*, which have sounds of their own that can be made both long and loud, then prolong them sensibly and firmly before the vowel. This may be indicated on the black board by doubling the initial of the following word. Thus (A. 13) incipiā, ffractī; (F. 8) cárpe díē, cquammínimū, ccrēdula posterō.[1]

ART. 93.—The rule *d* is also easy to carry out when once the effect of doubled consonants between vowels has been properly grasped. The difficulties arise first, from thus connecting together several distinct words, and consequently several syllables with raised pitch; secondly from the fact that the doubled consonant occurs in a syllable of low pitch, and often little force, *which has*

[puer] Cicerōnī placuisse *aiio maiinm*que gemināt I scrībere quod sī est, etiam jungētur ut consonans, (1, 4, 11), that is, if so, Cicero must have said aijō maija. As the plan is very reasonable it may be adopted without much hesitation, so that we should read (L. 20) as, jáijaffutū'rusrū'sticus.

[1] Thus I find in a curious Neapolitan version of the Aeneid by Giancola Sitillo, (Naples, 1784, lent me by Mr. Hodgson), in a translation of (A.), the following initial reduplications : che mme, lo ccomme, uocchie ssi, la parte cchiù, a mme, io nne, de la cchiù, a ffunno. These seem to imply this energy, but I am not sufficiently acquainted with the dialect to judge, having only heard very little of it more than thirty years ago.

nevertheless to be made sensibly long ; and thirdly, from the necessity of distinguishing, for example, tántus|spêrat, with two *s*'s, from tántum spêrat.= tántusspêrat with double *s*. Hence it will be necessary to practise detached combinations of words, still without regard to sense and in the singsong manner, until they can be executed with ease and precision, just like a troublesome passage in music. There is really no difficulty for an Englishman in any one of the sounds to be produced, because they are all existent in his own language. The sole difficulty exists in their being combined in an unusual manner.

ART. 94.—Practise first, final words, as : dolō′rē (A. 3) labō′rē (A. 11), fúrtī (A. 18), crē′do équidē (B. 4) which offer no difficulty except in remembering that the *m* has only to be regarded as a mark to shew that the preceding vowel is long.

Next, final words "energising" the next consonant, as already cited.

Then words with enclitics *ve*, as dolopūve (A. 7), and especially with enclitic *que*, as uterúcque (A. 20), legúcque (D. 9), sylvārúcque (I. 1), certácque (I. 10) pavidúcque (L. 17). The difficulty here is simply in not inserting the customary *m*.

ART. 95.—Lastly, the very common cases of joined words must be practised till they run with perfect ease from the tongue. Little phrases must be practised separately, or otherwise no good result will be obtained. Thus infándurrēgîna (A. 3) et quō′ruppárs mágna, myrmídonuddolopū′ve (A. 7), jánnóx (A. 8), (quite different from jánnox, in which the voice falls on the second syllable), ductō′rēs dánaū ttót jállābéntibus annīs (A. 14), instar móntis équū ddīvīnā pálladis árte (A. 15), (as this is a common example in grammars, it will be very difficult to correct the old bad habits of reading it), vō'tupprō réditū (A. 17) dēlécta vírū ssortī'ti (A. 18), dîves ópū, ppríamī (A. 22), nunc tántussínus (A. 23), quō féssurrápitis (B. 1), ingéntellū'ctū nnê quae're, *or* ingéntellū'ctunnê quae're (C. 1, practise both ways), hunc tántuffâta (C. 2), nímiū vōbīs (C. 3), quántōs ílle vírū mmágnammāvórtis adúrbē (C. 5), quúttúmulū ppraeterlabêre *or* quúttúmuluppraeterlabêre (C. 7, practise both, the last will be found difficult owing to the number of syllables necessarily kept in a low pitch), quísquaddēgénte (C. 8), intántusspê tóllet ávōs (C. 9), sê tántuttéllūs (C. 10), seu quúppédes īret (C. 13), purpúreōs spárgafflō'rēs animácque nepōtis hīs sálte‿accúmuleddōnīs.

Also try (HOR. *Od.* 3, 1, 5,)

> rē'guttimendō- ruin- própiōs greges,
> r'ēgēs in ípsōs impéri- uest- Jovis ;

out of which, by practice, a really majestic effect can be obtained. Dwell on the *dō* and run the *ru* very briefly on to the *in*, which, without being unduly emphasised or raised in pitch, must be fully lengthened. The *uest* following *ri*, will be found difficult at first.

The well-known line *Aen.* 3, 658, is merely a case of omitted *m* and slurred vowels, and is not likely to occasion difficulty, except perhaps in giving the high pitch to the first syllable in *īngens*, thus

> môn-stru̧hor-rén-du̧in-fór-mȩin-gens cúl-lûmen adémptū.

The following are also useful exercises :—

> tantus spērābat, tantus spērāverat hērōs ;
> tantum spērābam, tantum spērāveram et ipse.

Read the second line : tántusspērā'bā, ttántusspērā'veraet-ipse, and keep the *tusspē, bā ttan*, quite distinct from the *tus spē*, and *bat tan* of the other line, where the words will distinctly separate *s s* and *t t* as *two* letters, from the double letters *ss* and *tt*.

Distinguish, quī mūsam vīdit, mūsā vīdit mūsam ; as : quī mū'sau vī'dit, mūsā vī'dit mu'sā, which shews that the *mū'sau* means *mūsam* and the first *mūsā* therefore must be *mūsā* the ablative ("by means of the muse"), so that the last *mūsā* must be the accusative *mūsam*.

ART. 96.—These examples will serve to shew how the passages may be written on the black board by the teacher, for pronunciation by the pupil, after he has pronounced them himself several times to the class (Art. 19 note). All pronunciation is acquired by imitation, and it is not till after hearing a sound many times that we are able to grasp it sufficiently well to imitate. It is a mistake constantly made by teachers of language to suppose that a pupil knows by once hearing unfamiliar sounds, or even unfamiliar combinations of familiar sounds. When pupils are made to imitate too soon, they acquire an erroneous pronunciation, which they afterwards hear constantly from themselves actually or mentally, and believe that they hear from the teacher during the small fraction of a second that each sound lasts, and hence the habits of these organs become fixed. In the present case both teacher and pupil have been probably for years accustomed to attribute a different sound to *m* final, to give it the same sound in Latin *jam* as in English *jam*, and the utmost care and attention will be required to overcome this habit.

ART. 97.—It would be not a bad exercise to require pupils to write out Latin passages after the model of the preceding, indicating the words that are run on together by writing them together, marking the acute and circumflex accent always, together with the naturally long vowel, writing also the proper sound heard in place of *m* when it is sounded at all, and omitting it otherwise. Thus the passage (C.) would be thus written :—

ō nâte ingéntellū'ctū nnê quáère tuō'rū,
osténdent térrīs húnc tántuffâta, nequeúltrā
ésse sínent, nímiū vō'bīs rōmânapropā'gō
vīsa pótens, súperī, própriaháèc sīdō'na fuíssent.
quántōs ílle vírū, mmágnammāvórtis adúrbē
cámpus áget gémitūs, velquáè, tiberîne, vidêbis,
fúnera, quuttúmuluppraeterlābêre recéntē !
néc púer īlíacā quísquaddēgénte lātī'nōs
intántusspê tóllet ávōs, néc rómula quóndā
úllō sê tántuttéllūs [*or* tántū ttéllūs] jactābit alúmnō
héu píetās, héu prísca fídēs, invictáque béllō
déxtera ! nōn íllī sê quísquaimpûne tulísset
óbvius armā'tō, séu quúppédes īret inhóstē,
séu spūmántis équī fóderet calcā'ribus ármōs,
héu miseránde púer, sīquâ fâtaáspera rúmpās
tû marcéllus éris.   mánibus dáte lī'lia plē'nīs,
purpúreos spárgaffō'rēs, animácque nepótis
hîs sálteaccúmuleddō'nīs, et fúngar inā'nī
mū'nere.

The writing will fix the sounds and accents in the minds of the pupils.   Then several pupils should be called on in succession to read out what one has written, and the others should watch to check them, by ear only, without looking at the writing, which is best effected perhaps by turning the back of the blackboard to the listeners.   The master should be just as much on the watch for corrections to be made, as the pupils to make them, and should not be satisfied unless attention is drawn to the error, and the right sound is given, by some of the pupils. Once reached, the right pronunciation should be repeated over and over again correctly, to overcome the former vicious habit. A special study should be made of monosyllabic slurs and assimilations, as : túinténdens túrremíttens (M. 10), súadmīrâtus (R. 9). Few perhaps would not hesitate at first over the line quoted from Horace in Art. 90 ; committēs rêómneet vi'taet cuccórpore fā'mā, as it must be read at first for mere metre. Afterwards the *et*'s will be more separated as : rêómne, et vīta, et cuccórpore.

Art. 98.—A purely scholastic question, of some importance however, arises from teaching grammar to boys. How is the presence of the unpronounced *m* to be marked? Should not boys be made to pronounce it, to shew the teacher that they know it to be present? If a boy repeats *amābā*, how is the teacher to know that the boy knows the word to be written *āmābam* ? Let the classical master remember English. How does the pupil know that *thou art, you are*, are spelled as they are, when he speaks the *ou* in *thou* and *you* quite differently, and the *ar* without any *e* in *art* in the same way as the *are* in *you are*, which has an *e*? If the commonest " school board " children and teachers get over this difficulty, what is to be expected from " classical school " children and teachers? Again let the classical master consult his colleague the French teacher. When a boy repeats in French, je sui, tu é, il è, nou som, vouzèt, ilson ; how does he know of the existence of the numerous consonants, which on occasion may be very active, as je suis ici, il sont ici ? Or let him ask himself how, on the present plan of barbaric English Latin pronunciation, the boy knows that *vitium* has *t, convīcium* has *c,*

Elysium has *s*, when he hears English *sh* in all? The boy learns Latin by *eye* chiefly, and hence knows the *m* from the first, and his main difficulty consists, not in forgetting its presence, but in recollecting it too well. However, the master has an easy plan in speech. Let the boy say : amābam ego, amābam tē, amābam vōs, amābam mātrem. If he uses the same *amābā* in all cases, he does not know that the word ends in *m*. But if he says : amābaégo, amā'battê, amā'-bauvôs, amā'bammā'trē, (not amā'bam mā'trem) he may be trusted to have a right mental vision of the spelling. It is right, however, that teachers should remember that for this one new difficulty, which is felt as a difficulty only because it is new, thousands of facilitations, orthographical, grammatical, etymological and metrical, would be introduced by the quantitative system of pronunciation.

VIII. Elegiac and Lyric Verse Rhythm.

ART. 99.—By this time the pupils should have overcome all rhythmical difficulties of pronunciation so far as length of syllable and pitch accent is concerned. But it will always be safest to exercise the pupil in the singsong fashion and with the pendulum, to acquire any new metre, slowly at first to make sure of each syllable, and then rapidly. The following remarks apply to the acquisition of new metrical systems.

ART. 100.—After hexameters proceed to choriambic verses. These have generally a spondee or iambus to begin and an iambus to end. (E.) and (F.) are very instructive. Observe in (F.) how the division of the

words varies the three choriambi in each line, except in
(F. 5,) and note the consequent monotony of that line.

ART. 101.—Pentameters are best studied as choriambic, consisting of two halves, composed (as I view
them) each of a dactyle and choriambus, varying into
a spondee and molossus in the first half only. Observe
also the great difference of the pitch rhythm in older
writers, as Propertius (G.), and the stereotyped Ovidian
cadence in (H.), where the pentameter must end in a dissyllable, of which the last syllable comparatively seldom
ends in a short open vowel. Nothing serves to shew the
great difference of feeling in Greek and Latin rhythm more
than the treatment of the final half of a pentameter line.

ART. 102.—Both the Sapphic and Alcaic stanzas, in
(I.) and (K.), also sound to me principally choriambic.
In the Sapphic, the choriamb is preceded by a compound
foot, called a second epitrite, consisting of a trochee and
spondee, and as a general rule a word ends with the
first syllable of the choriamb (which would therefore have
a low pitch). though sometimes it ends with the *second*
syllable, as in (I. 1, 9, 10.) The common English
"swing" with which these verses are read is simply
atrocious.[1] Even the final short line gives me the feeling

---

[1] The ordinary swing of English reading of sapphics quite disregards quantity
and the Latin laws of pitch-accent, but substitutes for them other quantities and
other pitches. It is not possible to give the English sounds in Latin letters, but
I can fancy Maecenas on waking, after 1900 years' sleep, in an English school,
attempting to write the English pronunciation of (I. 2—8), somewhat in this
way ; the final italic *m* indicating that it was heard :

lū´sidem sī´lai dī´kesoco lé´ndai
sem´peret k´ol´tai, dē´ tiquipri kĕ´´mer
tém´pori sĕ´krŏ.
quŏ´sibi lấi´nai mŏn´niuīri vér´sius
vér´zinīz léc´tas piú´erŏsqui cás tŏs
dấi´squaibes sé´ptem plác´iuīri kŏl´līz
dấi´siri lŏ´´dīs.

of the central choriamb, with a syllable over, rather than of a dactyle and spondee.

ART. 103.—The same choriamb or its equivalent molossus, which were both very common combinations in Latin speech, seem also, to me, to give their own peculiar character to the Alcaic stanza.   Thus in (K.) the choriambs : prōpositī, prava juben- | tium, men-te quatit-, tur-bidus had- | riae, mag-na manus-, im-pavidum-, and the molossī : in-stan-tis-, il-lābātur, are (to me) the pith of the rhythm, the rest is accessory.   This of course is far from being the usual view.

ART. 104.—Iambic verses come next to prose, and may be studied in Horace, or Phaedrus, to escape the ancient comic writers, Terence and Plautus, where the rhythm was so difficult to seize even by Augustan Romans, that Cicero felt the necessity of a piper to make him feel it (O. 13-15), and Horace could not scan Plautus, even on his fingers, as we learn by his saying to the Pīsōnēs (*Ars. Poet.* 270—274) :—

> at vestrī proavī Plautīnōs et numerōs et
> laudāvēre salēs, nimium patienter utrúmque,
> nē dīcam stultē mīrātī ; sī modo ego et vōs
> scīmus inurbānum lepidō sēpōnere dictō,
> lēgitimúmque sonum digitīs callēmus et aure.

Of course he would have no conception that the words were those of his old friend Horace, in a metre invented by Sappho, and it would be real cruelty to enlighten his darkness.   The remarkable parts of this method of reading are, the foot of four syllables, the first having both the force and pitch accent, and the last three just audible, and the uniform singsong of the pitch.   Such feet and such swing occur only in English sapphics, as in this stanza from Canning's well-known *Needy Knifegrinder.*

> I'· should be | glád· to | drínk· your honour's | héalth· in
> A'· pot of | béer, if | yóu· would give me | six· pence,
> Bút· for my | párt·, I | név·er love to | méd· dle
>   With· poli | tics·, sir.

Here English accents are magnificently procrusteanised to fit into the schoolboy's rhythm.   "O, reform it altogether !"

ART. 105.—The putative resemblance of the Latin Iambic to the ordinary English vérse occasions much difficulty to an Englishman, because it constantly misleads him into violations of the laws of quantity.[1] It is also difficult to mark the time in Iambic verse, because the length of each foot is generally not constant. In Catullus we have indeed examples of pure Iambic verses in the poems—

> iv. phasēlus ille quem vidētis, hospitēs
>   ait fuisse nāvium celerrimus.

xxvii. (xxix.) quis hōc potest vidēre, quis potest patī
        nisi‿impudīcus et vorāx et āleō?

But generally a spondee was allowed in the first, third, or fifth foot. The effect of these spondees requires careful consideration. That it was very marked and important is clear from the words of Horace who calls the iamb a "rapid foot," and says that originally every foot in the sēnārius was an iamb, but that "not long since," the verse admitted "steady spondees" to make the lines "slower and more solemn," but that Accius seldom used this liberty, although Ennius either from carelessness or

---

[1] English verse is not *regulated* by the *length* of the syllables it contains, as Latin verse is; although *length* of syllables frequently produces rhythmical effects, which shew the master hand, just as pitch-accents *embellish* Latin rhythm. If we consider that the names of Latin *feet* refer to combinations of *long* and *short* syllables exclusively, then it will be seen how inappropriate they are to English *measures*, or combinations of *strong* and *weak* syllables exclusively (using these adjectives as expressing *greater* and *smaller* amounts of *force*). If we persist in using an iamb in English for the measure of a weak syllable followed by a strong one, as *awa·ke*, and appropriate the other names in the same way, let us at least prefix such a term as *force*, and speak of *awa·ke* being a *force-iamb*; *slee·per* a *force-trochee*, *ver·ity* a *force-dactyle*, and so on. Or, to avoid repetition, preface any such use of the names of feet by the notice: "names of *quantitative feet* are here employed solely for *force-measures*." There is more than a mere question of name here. The application of the old name to the new case arose from an absolute confusion of ideas, which the continuance of the custom perpetuates.

ignorance of his art allowed his lines to be "oppressed" by spondees. The whole passage is of great importance as shewing the sensible effect of spondees as contrasted with iambs.[1] The iamb itself, by merely resolving its long syllable into two short, might be replaced by a tribrach, in all places but the last, and the spondee by a dactyle or anapest. This occasions the difficulty in counting time, for the number of short lengths in a foot was variable. In (L. 1, 7) we have pure iambics, the only cases in this example. One spondee occurs in (L. 2, 3, 4, 6, 8, 9, 10, 11, 12, 14, 16, 18, 19.) Two spondees occur in (L. 5, 13, 15, 20, 21, 22.) A tribrach is found in (L. 8) jacē | re modo, and (L. 17) pavidúm | que lepo | re^m. A dactyle occurs in (L. 14) aut ami | te. And two anapests as well as a tribrach and a slur occur in (L. 17) pavidúm | que lepo | re^m et ad | venam | laqueō | gruem, and one of these occurs very unusually in the fifth foot.

ART. 106.—Phaedrus allows iamb, tribrach, spondee, dactyle or anapest in any place, except the last. The comedians are even more dreadful. The effect to me is

---

[1] syllaba longa brevī subjecta vocătur iambus,
pēs citus; unde etiam trimetrīs accrescere jūssit
nōmen iambēīs, quum sēnōs redderet ictūs
prīmus ad extrēmum similis sibi : *nōn ita prīdem
tardior* ut paulō *graviōr*que venīret ad aurēs,
spondēōs stabilēs in jūra paterna recēpit
commodus et patiens, nōn ut dē sēde secundā
cēderet aut quartā sociăliter. hīc et in Accī
nōbilibus trimetrīs *appāret rārus,* et Ennī
in scēnam missōs cum magnō pondere versūs
aut operae celeris nimium cūrāque carentis,
aut ignōrātae *premit* artis crīmine turpī.

A. P. 251—262.

Observe here the use of ictūs as denoting a metrical interval, and the implication that the length of these intervals varied when the spondee was introduced, with which compare Quint. 9, 4, 51, who speaks of intervals between the beats (percussiōnes) of four and five units (σημεῖα), so that classical time-keeping was very different from our conductor's *bâton.* See (Art. 14).

then merely prose spoiled—with neither the melody of
verse nor the fine flow of prose,—reminding me forcibly
of my own boyish attempts at blank verse, when I considered it to be simply prose chopped up into lengths of
ten syllables.   This may be very unscholarlike, but it is
a comfort to err on such a point with Cicero and Horace.
If the older writers had a really intelligible metre (as we
cannot but believe they had), then their language and its
pronunciation were entirely different from the Augustan
Latin (which is otherwise extremely probable), and we
have not as yet acquired a sufficient insight into it.   The
English scansions I have heard attempted vīvā vōce,
were simply impossible and intolerable, and emendations
proposed upon the hypothesis of their correctness are to
me by that very hypothesis discredited.   There was the
same feeling at one time respecting Chaucerian metres,
till a key to his pronunciation was found.   We must
wait for a similar key to Plautus and Terence.   At least
I have not found it in Corssen.   At present then I can
only recommend these older writings to be read in the
Augustan pronunciation as semi-versified *prose*,—knowing
indeed that this must be considerably wrong, but feeling
that it cannot be so dreadfully wrong as our present
habits.   Reading Phaedrus rhythmically may be a useful
introduction.   He certainly felt the rhythm himself, or he
could not have commenced by saying

> Aesōpus auctor quam māteriam repperit
> hanc ego *polīvī* versibus sēnāriīs !

The first line, with its dactyle in the fourth place
(whence Horace refuses to oust the iamb) is a study in
itself.   The number of feet and the final iamb are the
only remaining marks of the iambic trimeter.

IX. Prose Rhythm.

ART. 107.—Prose is the most difficult thing to read in any language. We allow much to the swing of verse, but if the prose reader does not bring out the eloquence of the original, and make all the points as he goes on, pronouncing purely, accurately, and distinctly, and preserving the national custom of intonation, at the same time, we think little of him. The passages quoted from Cicero in the Appendix (M., N., O., P., Q., R.), will serve to show the extreme importance which he attributed to *prose rhythm* and to its clear separation from *verse rhythm.*

ART. 108.—It is curious to see him in (M.) finding the Latin system of intonation the only natural one. The Latins and Greeks indeed agreed in not placing the highest pitch at a greater distance than the third syllable from the end, but the Greeks allowed it on the last syllable, (as in the word in O. 9) and the Latins, at least in Quintilian's time, did not.[1] . Still the absolute fixity of the Latin custom is proved by Cicero's view that it was natural. In (R.) we have it confirmed by the story of Gracchus's piper, in (N.) the same steady observance of quantity is shewn, and in (O.) and (P.) it appears that in prose as well as in (at least iambic) verse, rhythm was

---

[1] See the decisive passages quoted from Quintilian (Art. 41 note). When Priscian admits the accent to be placed on the last syllable "discrētiōnis causā," his *accentus* was no longer Quintilian's *tenor*, and Cicero's *acūta et gravis vōx.* Hence all the indications cited by Corssen (II. 808, et sqq.) are inapplicable to Augustan pronunciation, that is, to our present investigation. There is nothing so unscientific in historical investigations of pronunciation, as the confusion of periods. No attempt should be made to venture on this dangerous ground in our imitations of Augustan Latin.

chiefly regulated by the quantity of the few syllables
towards the close of a clause.

ART. 109.—In other places Cicero cautions the
speaker of prose from falling into verse. Thus quoting
Aristotle approvingly with a slight change, he says (*Or.*
§ 194) :

> Iambus enim et dactylus in versum cadunt maximē; itáque ut
> versum fugimus in ōrātiōne, sīc hī sunt ēvītandī continuātī pedēs.
> Aliud enim quiddam est ōrātiō, nec quidquam inimīcius quam illa
> versibus. Paeōn autem minimē est aptum ad versum ; quō liben-
> tius eum recēpit ōrātiō.

And then, from himself he says (*Ib.* § 195) :

> Ego autem sentiō, omnēs in ōrātiōne esse quasi permīstōs et con-
> fūsōs pedēs. Nec enim effugere possēmus animadversiōnem, sī
> semper īsdem ūterēmur. Quia neque numerōsa esse, ut poēma ;
> neque extrā numerum, ut sermō vulgī est, dēbet esse ōrātiō. Al-
> terum nimis est vinctum, ut dē industriā factum appāreat : alterum
> nimis dissolūtum, ut pervagātum, ac vulgāre videātur : ut ab alterō
> nōn dēlectēre, alterum ōderis. Sit igitur permista et temperāta
> numerīs, nec dissolūta nec tōta numerōsa. Paeōne maximē (quo-
> niam optimus auctor ita censet) sed reliquīs etiam numerīs quōs
> ille praeterit, temperāta.

The paeōn has three short syllables and one long,
differently distributed, and Cicero really dissents from
Aristotle as to its use (P. 9, 10). No doubt this depended on the difference between Greek and Latin
intonation. The great value of these passages to us is
to shew that quantity was the only recognized guide to
rhythm in prose and verse. Quintilian thoroughly
agrees with Cicero's view, saying :

> In compositiōne ōrātiōnis certior et magis omnium aperta servāri
> dēbet *dīmensiō*. Est igitur in pedibus, (9, 4, 52.) Ratiō verō pedum in

ōrātiōne est multō quam in versū difficilior : prīmum quod versus
paucīs continētur, ōrātiō longiōrēs habet saepe circuitūs [never
'circu*m*itūs,' see p. 65] : deinde quod versus semper similis sibi
est et ūnā ratiōne [unaltered measurement] dēcurrit, ōrātiōnis
compositiō, nisi varia est, et offendit simultūdine et in affectātiōne
dēprehenditur.   Et in omnī quidem corpore tōtōque (ut ita dixerim)
tractū numerus insertus est.   Neque enīm loquī possumus nisi syllabīs
brevibus āc longīs, ex quibus pedēs fīunt (9, 4, 60. 61.)

ART. 110.—To teach a person to read prose *well* even
in his own language is difficult, partly because he has
seldom heard prose well read, though he is constantly
hearing prose spoken around him, intonated, but unrhythmical.   In the case of a dead language, like the
Latin, which the pupil never hears spoken, and seldom
hears read, except by himself or his equally ignorant and
hobbling fellow-scholars, this difficulty is inordinately
increased.   Let me once more impress on every teacher
of Latin the *duty* of himself learning to read Latin
readily according to accent and quantity ; the *duty* of his
reading out to his pupils, of his setting them a *pattern*,[1]
of his hearing that they follow it, of his correcting their
mistakes, of his *leading* them into right habits.   If the
quantitative pronunciation be adopted, no one will be fit
to become a classical teacher who cannot read a simple
Latin sentence decently with a strict observance of that
quantity by which alone the greatest of Latin orators
regulated his own rhythms.   We have by this time also
probably learned to acknowledge that the introduction
of a pitch accent, that is, the elevation of the pitch of
the voice on the so-called accented syllable, and its de-
pression on the other syllables, even in interrogative
sentences, is quite as essential to the feeling of that part

---

[1] See Art. 19, note, and Art. 96.

of Latin rhythm which depends upon caesūra, or the
division of words; and that the adoption of our English
freedom of pitch, or rising inflection in questions, must
have been as disagreeable to an Augustan Roman, as the
Scotch or French intonation of English is to a Londoner.
Think how Shakspere's lines would fall from the mouth
of a Frenchman! There are some Frenchmen (as
Fechter) that give our English rhythms far better than
we English can hope to give the Latin rhythms; but even
in them we at once detect the foreign intonation which
destroys the genuine roll, as we like to hear it—though
certainly our own modern speech would have been very
thin and poor, effeminate and affected, in Shakspere's
own ears. But only fancy a Frenchman declaiming
Shakspere with his own values of the vowels, his own
curious use of the force and pitch accent and emphasis,
his own treatment of quantity, and his own intonation!
Would not every Englishman stop his ears and flee?
And this is but a faint shadow of the atrocious manner in
which we have hitherto dared to treat Virgil and Horace
and Cicero!

ART. 111.—My remarks have been directed to the
case of a transition, where the pupils have been hitherto
accustomed to our vile English pronunciation of Latin,
and I have also taken into consideration the difficulties
which the teachers themselves have to overcome in
unlearning the old and learning the new. When the
teachers are able to read with instinctive fluency, and
begin with young boys, making them read by quantity
and pitch from the first, the whole matter is much sim-
plified. Care should be taken that all long vowels are
properly marked in the school books. There is no

occasion to mark unpronounced or assimilated *m*, or the
short vowels; and I cannot sufficiently reprobate the
usual custom of marking a *vowel* as long, when all we
know is that the *syllable* containing it is long, owing to
a concurrence of consonants (see Art. 23, note). The
teacher must carefully read out the words to be learned.
He has to become a teacher of reading, and must recognise the responsibilities and difficulties of that office. Of
course, such teaching begins with prose—and very prosy
unrhythmical prose; but the length and pitch of each
syllable can be scrupulously observed even in declining,
mūsa, mū′sae, and conjugating, ámō, ámās, ámat. Indeed
if a pupil can regularly and securely mark the pitch
accent and quantity in every form of the usual paradigms
given in grammars, he will have very little difficulty in
what follows. But when boys are allowed to say (using
Latin letters to express our English pronunciation):
ēmō· ēmas· ēmat· ēmē·mes ēmē·tis ēman·t, ēmēbam·
ēmēbas· ēmēbat· am-ebē·mes am-ebē·tis ēmēban·t, and so
on, the master is laying up a store of difficulties for the
future (see Art. 35; see also Art. 98.)

ART. 112.—The great question for an Englishman is,
what shall he do with his own force accent? The
answer is pretty much the same as for French—Put it by,
and say as little about it as possible. An Englishman
cannot avoid, and has no occasion to avoid, speaking
some syllables forcibly and emphatically; but he must
never allow that force, as in his own language, to alter
the relative length or pitch of the syllables, or the purity
of the vowel sounds. Taking these precautions, at-
tending most scrupulously to these points, he may do
pretty well what he pleases with the force accent. How,

when the feeling for quantity dimn.ed, pitch accents became gradually converted into force accents, does not
concern us at present, for we must suppose that quantity
and pitch accent are in full force, and must make them
live in our imitation of Augustan speech.[1]   It will be

[1] The feeling for quantity seems to have gone first, while the consciousness of
the accented syllable remained. The nature of the accent then became indifferent.
Possibly raised pitch and increased force had for some time gone regularly
together, and as their combination required greater exertion, this very effort
assisted in impairing the feeling for quantity. The modern Greek, the modern
Italian, and modern Spaniard, seem not to know the meaning of fixed quantity.
In their languages quantity is now as variable as pitch, but force is fixed upon
certain syllables.   Corssen (II. 942) quotes some Latin hexameters of the latter
part of the *third* century, in which it is evident that all feeling for quantity had
died out.   In my paper on *Accent and Quantity* (Philol. Trans. 1873—4, p. 153),
I have compared these with lines of Virgil which have almost the same rhythm
of force accents as they would have been read with at Eton when I was there
(1830—3).   The same result remains if we use the Augustan pronunciation,
neglecting distinctions of quantity, but preserving the place of the force accent.
I add the comparison here, representing the force accent by a turned period as
usual, and omitting all marks of quantity and pitch accent. And I also add
some English lines (of about the same calibre, that is, nearly "nonsense verses,")
but of precisely the same rhythmical construction, which may facilitate the comparison. The hexameter lines, I. to V. are subdivided because the force rhythm
is thus better exhibited. The numbers 1, 2, 3, refer to the original, the English,
and the Virgilian lines : —

> I. 1. Praefa·tio nos·tra
>   2. Irra·tional doc·trines,
>   3. Excu·tior som·no, et
>
>   1. vi·am erran·ti demon·strat,
>   2. held·-by believ·ers as-per·fect,
>   3. sum·mi fasti·gia lecti.—*Ae.* 2, 302.
>
> II. 1. Respectum·que bo·num,
>   2. Are-but-ar·rant fol·lies
>   3. Praesentem·que vi·ris
>
>   1. cum-ve·nerit sae·culi me·ta,
>   2. to-those·-who-have stud·ied-the sub·ject.
>   3. inten·tant om·nia mor·tem.—*Ae.* 1, 91.
>
> III. 1. Aeter·num fi·eri,
>   2. Misfor·tune teach·es-us
>   3. Carpe·bant, hy·ali
>
>   1. quod-discre·dunt in·scia cor·da.
>   2. that-the-best·-are of·ten-in er·ror.
>   3. sat·uro fuca·ta colo·ri.—*Geo.* 4, 335.

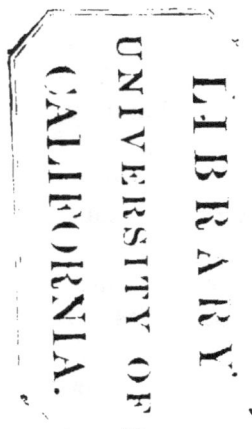

found that much effect is often given by a force accent
on a syllable with depressed pitch ; and at least as much
variety can be produced by judicious variations of force
in Latin, as we give in English by judicious variations of
pitch.

X. How to Read Late Latin.

ART. 113.—A question arises as to the proper method
of reading late Latin, written and pronounced by the
writers without attention to pitch accent or to quantity.
The answer is very simple.   Only one pronunciation can
be taught in schools, and that should be the best imitation we can obtain of the Augustan Latin.   If we admitted the principle of using the pronunciation of the
later writers, we should probably have to learn a mul-
titude of different pronunciations—at least one for each
century, and one for each native country of the writer.

        IV. 1. E·go simil·iter
             2. E·ven nobil·ity
             3. Qua·lis popu·lea

             1. erra·vi tem·pore mul·to
             2. of·heart·-and soul·-may-be cheat·ed.
             3. mae·rens philome·la sub um·bra.—*Geo.* 4, 511.

        V. 1. Fa·na prosequen·do,
             2. Sense·less adora·tion
             3. Hu·jus odora·to

             1. paren·tibus in·sciis ipsis.
             2. of·all·-that-is old·-is-the key·stone.
             3. radi·ces in·coque Baccho.—*Geo.* 4, 279.

It is evident that it is our *ratio* and not our *aurēs* which, on the old plan of
reading, would find the first lines of these triplets full of false quantities, and the
third lines proper hexameters.   But read them by the rules of Augustan pronunciation, and Virgil's lines have a regular appreciable rhythm, while the
others become a mere jumble.   It is evident then that we can learn nothing of
Augustan usages from the *tertiary* strata which produced the above hideous
fossils.   In the words of the accentual hexameter I, " viam erranti dēmonstrant,"
they shew the way you're not to go !

ART. 114.—As far as prose is concerned, there is
evidently no objection to using as near an approach to
Ciceronian speech as we can compass.   As regards all
literary verse, it is written on Augustan models down to
yesterday's school exercises all over the world, and cannot
be read rhythmically except in Augustan pronunciation.
It may indeed not be possible to read it rhythmically at
all, but that is the fault of the author's skill, not of his intention.   On the other hand, medieval hymns (Art. 57)
and other Latin verses, like Father Prout's

> Quam pul·cra sunt o·va
> Cum tos·ta et no·va
>   E stab·ulo sci·te legun·tur,
> Et a Mar·gery bel·la,
> Quae festi·va puel·la !
>   Pin·guis lar·di cum frus·tris coquun·tur,

may be read with force accents only, without regard to
quantity or slurring, and with English final *m*, but otherwise with the pronunciation of the letters here assumed.
It is only in merely farcical mixtures of English and
Latin, or some other modern language and Latin, that
the pronunciation of the modern language has to be
adopted, but with these we have really nothing to do.

XI. Final Method of Reading Latin.

ART. 115.—After the pupil has thus acquired the full
feeling of the rhythmical construction of any passage by
learning to feel the length and musical pitch of its
syllables, he has to clothe this bare skeleton with living
flesh and make it talk Augustan sense in Augustan

speech. Of course a perfect comprehension of the passage and its bearings is necessary for this purpose, and some theory must be formed of the Augustan method of intonating phrases as well as words, and of general delivery (actiō, prōnuntiātiō). On this point there is much to read in Cicero and Quintilian with which a teacher should become familiar. But through all varieties of tone (omnēs sonōrum gradūs, M. 9) the reader must bear in mind relative quantity and relative pitch so far as the syllables of a single word are concerned. He must be, as an Englishman, particularly careful *not* to raise his voice on the last syllables of exclamations and questions as in : ē'jà ! quíd stā'tìs? (D. 18, 19) which he will be very apt to read : ē'já ! quìd stā'tís?

ART. 116.—It is recommended that short pieces should be gradually practised perfectly. The younger pupils, who have not the power of mind or experience to originate for themselves, should follow patterns set by the teacher (Art. 19), and committed to memory by the pupil. So far as verse is concerned, a power of repeating from memory the examples in the Appendix will be of great service. I have found that by constantly repeating them, either mentally or aloud (as in country walks), with the best methods of delivery I could call up, I have gained more knowledge of the possible *life* of Augustan poetry, than I ever possessed during my school days at Shrewsbury and Eton, or my college days at Cambridge. And I have thus been able to convert dead signs into real living sounds, such as may have moved the hearts and thoughts of men of old.

ART. 117.—The prose part of the examples is deficient in passages of varied feeling and declamation; it is almost entirely didactic. My wish was to give the most important words of the most important writer who had treated of prose rhythm, and to shew by them the complete subservience of Augustan prose rhythm to quantity. But the reader will find no difficulty in turning up passages in Cicero's orations or Livy's histories, which involve the highest declamatory powers, while the familiar letters of Cicero may be read as actual communications with his friends, and his " Terentiā et Tulliolā duābus animīs suīs."

ART. 118.—In reading the paper on which the present tract is founded, I delivered the whole of the following passages in the most varied way I could compass, not, as I explained, for the purpose of shewing off my own powers of reading, but to enable the classical teachers then present, to realise. if but for a short time, my notion of the nature of living Augustan Latin in its various phases, in its various moods, tones, pitches, qualities of voice, in short, to bring back, so far as I could conceive it, the old *ring* of Augustan speech, and to shew that my rules were not dead pedantry, but a living breath. I think, therefore, that it may be convenient to add a few remarks on the way in which I endeavoured to read these examples, as a guide to the teacher who wishes to use them as patterns for his own pupils.

ART. 119.—And first I would observe, that, at least in my day, a schoolboy's repetitions were " gabbled ; " that the master's sole interest seemed to be that the boy should shew he remembered the words, without any regard to sense or style of delivery ; a falsely-placed accent (styled a " false quantity ") might be observed and punished, but nothing else. The dreary drone, the hesitation, the repetition of words, the humming and hawing, the cast-down eyes, the depressed figure, the weary tone, are dismal recollections of my youth.   Now we do not want to make actors or orators of the boys, but we should make them read decently, intelligibly, with the just sound of each syllable both in length and pitch, and if possible, with an indication of the characteristic quality of tone by which joy and grief, rage and joke, argument and feeling, are distinguished.   More has to be done for "speech days" of course, but I am talking of ordinary repetition, which should be made a lesson in distinct utterance, and for that purpose the speaker should be placed as far off as possible from the master,—not close to him, as so often happens when a boy is " called up," a custom partly due to our inherited habit of hearing many classes at once in one large hall, instead of in separate rooms, — so that the master can carry out Quintilian's recommendations :—

Imprīmīs vitia sī qua sunt ōris [of pronunciation] ēmendet, ut ēxpressa sint verba, ut suīs quaeque litterae sonīs ēnuntientur.   Cūrā-bit etiam, nē ēxtrēmae syllabae intercidant ; ut pār sibi sermō sit ; ut recta sit faciēs dīcentis, nē labra distorqueantur, nē immodicus hiātus rictum discindat, nē supīnus vultus, nē dējectī in terram oculī, inclīnāta utrōlibet cervīx.   Nam frons plūribus generibus peccat. Vīdī multōs, quōrum supercilia ad singulōs vōcis cōnātūs allevāren-tur, aliōrum constricta, aliōrum etiam dissidentia, cum alterum in verticem tenderent, alterō paene oculus ipse premerētur (1, 11, 4. 8. 9—11).

Boys we see have not much changed since Quintilian's time.   I have myself seen in English schools every fault he mentions, and no doubt every classical teacher will recognise the picture.   But he should do more.   He should paint it out.

XII. How to Read the Poetical Examples in the Appendix.

ART. 120.—Bring out the character of each foot and each line distinctly, but gently, with a slight flexion of voice, never degenerating into a regular chant, and never interfering with the sense. Study a few lines at a time, and repeat them till you are quite perfect. This is essential at first, as otherwise bad habits will be acquired which can scarcely be thrown off. The grand sonorous swing of the Virgilian hexameter, the prettiness of the Ovidian elegiac, the playfulness or intenseness of the Horatian lyrics, the colloquiality of the satirical hexameter and iambics, must all be characterised, and all be well distinguished from prose by their unmistakable " pede certō."

ART. 121. *Example A.*—The two first lines are prose in sense and verse in form. They must be spoken rhythmically, but levelly, quietly, very distinctly, and without the least haste, as an evident prologue to what follows. In (1) conticuêreómnēs, the *con-* must be distinctly long, the pitch of the voice must be kept low till *ê* and then allowed to rise and fall again. Two English faults must here be guarded against ; no sound of *i*, or indistinct English *u* should follow *ē*, or be inserted before *r*, which should come clearly down upon *e* in *re* continuing the descent of the voice, but the syllable *re* is held for a very short time, and the pitch rises at once for *óm*. The *nēs* should be full, clear, low, and strong, and there should be no degradation of *s* into *z*. The following molossus *intentî* must have the two first syllables kept at a low pitch, so that the line is made very quiet by the three long low syllables *nēs inten.* Observe that the pitch rises and falls on the last syllable *tî* of the spondee, and in the syllable *queô*, it has first a low, then a high, and finally a low pitch.

The rhythm of (2) is brought out by dividing: índetórō páteraenē'ās sîc órsusabáltō. Be particular in the opening choriamb, giving full length to the first and last syllables. Run the *páter* shortly and clearly on the *aenē'as*, and be very careful in keeping *pa* short and *ae* long. We are so accustomed to talk of *pē·tərinī·əs* (where ə indicates our peculiar vowel in final *-er*), that much practice is necessary to overcome the difficulty. Mind that *sîc* is English *seek*, not English *sick.*

Lines (3—13) are an excuse. ⌠Aeneas is full of painful reminiscences.⌡ He begins slowly, in a dull voice: ínfándurrēgī'na; mind the opening long *īn*, and the assimilated *m.* This double *rr* is a difficulty to be much practised. Mind the long *rē;* there is a great tendency to shorten it. In (4) mind the molossus *trōjā'nās*, and the anapest *utópēs*, and then the three long low syllables *et lāmen* with the mournful rise on *tā'* (be sure not to say *lam* or *tab*). The choriamb and anapest which open (5): ērúerint dánaī, will occasion difficulty; they must be quite mournful, with the long *ē* well brought out; the voice rises for an instant, on *rú dá*, and the main expression is obtained by sinking the voice on the final long *ī.* The opening mournfulness continues to this point. Then, Aeneas thinks of himself and his voice becomes firmer. In the end of (5), *ípse* and *misérrima* have to be especially marked, the last most; in (6) *mágna* is the chief word, but be careful with the assimilated *m*, the trilled *r*, and the hard *s* in : quē'ṛuppárs. In *fŭi* the quantitative iamb must be well brought out without any tendency to a force-spondee, and the *ĭ* made long and low, without particular force.

In (6—8) another chord is struck. The tale of woe is so sad that *even* Myrmidons and Dolopes, and *harsh* Ulysses' men would weep over it. Bring out the reference to these points, and especially emphasise *dūrī* (7). Line (8) begins with a dactyle and choriamb, it is much like (4), the voice *sinks* on the *mīs* of lácrymīs, not *rises*, although interrogative. The *ā* must be kept long and low, without any force.

Lines 8 and 9 merely continue the excuses for not telling the story which is forthwith continued through two books of the Aeneid. The tone implies—"and you see that it's so late to-night, there will not be time." Care must be taken with *jánnóx*, with the long *prae* in *praecípitat*, and the pure *t* in *cadéntia*.

In (10, 11) we have a broken sentence, the verb is missing. Begin with *sed*, *sī*, as quite distinct syllables, bringing out the initial spondee ; *tántus* is the chief word ; in (11) *bréviter* (with careful *er* in *erring* not *ər*, and well trilled *r*), must have a little force. Take breath after trōjae to allow of uniting *sup-rē'muaudīre-labō'rē*, with a little emphasis on *suprē'mu*. Observe that the slurred vowels *uau* are all in low pitch. In (12) bring out the *hórret*, making its second syllable, as well as the following *lŭctū*, very long, and lead up to *refūgit*. Take breath after *animus*, and *horret*. Make a little pause after *refūgit*, and speak the *incípiā*, with the tone of a victim to circumstances, making *n* in *in* very long, *cí* clearly high pitched but short, and the *ā* rather indifferent. Then pause.

Begin the narrative (13) in a quiet and altered tone. Aeneas has now made up his mind to unbosom, and does so without stint. The two first lines (13, 14) are very quiet therefore, but observe *ffrácti* to compensate for omitted *m*, and oppose distinctly, but very quietly the two sentiments, *ffráctībéllō* (keeping *ī* and *ō* quite long) and *fātī'squerepúlsī* (*fā* and *tīs* both quite long). In (15) bring out *móntis*, but let *éqūu* be quiet, while the three last words *ddīvī'nā pálladis árte* (with *dd*) are parenthetical, and spoken with a tone implying that the Greeks could not have done it without such assistance. In (16) keep the first *ae* quite long, and observe *ábjete* for *abíete*, the position of high pitch being changed with the change of *ie* into *je* for the sake of the verse, compare Quintilian on *volúc-rēs* in Art. 24, note.

Line (17) is also parenthetical. The first clause is spoken with a kind of contempt for the trap into which the Trojans fell. The *éafáma vagátur*, is a mere *obiter dictum*, and, though important to the subsequent narrative, must be passed over lightly.

Lines (18—20) are simple narrative. Observe *vírū*, and guard against English *vir-*, also *ss* in *ssortī'tī* to compensate for omitted *m*. Be careful with the molossī, *inclūdunt* (19), and *ingéntēs* (20).

In (21) a completely new subject is taken up. The first words are as quiet as a guide book, and the difficulty consists in giving the many spondees their full length, when they convey so little matter. But just for that reason I consider this line to be one of the most useful quantitative exercises here given, and it should be well studied. The short *té* with high pitch is very trying, because it begins a significant word, and the chief importance must be given to its final low-pitched but long syllable *dos*, with short vowel. In (22) mind *divesópū*, and the following parenthesis, which must be spoken with a special reference to ancient splendor, and thus contrasted with (23) which shews the mournful results of its wreck. Pause after *nunc*, make *tántum* important, and *sínus* short and distinct, without separation, *tántussínus*, except by the raised pitch. The long *o* in *státiō* gives this word its chief force.

Lines (24) and (25) require no notice beyond what they have already received (Arts. 47, 49, 58*c*, 60.) They join on the description of Tenedos to the following narrative.

ART. 122. *Example B.*—Although these are consecutive lines in the original they belong to two distinct subjects, and have been introduced especially for the sake of (2). Anchises has been passing in review a large number of the future heroes of Rome, and had been asking how he could omit naming this one and that, when he sees the Fabiī, and asks how far they would lead him in his weariness, so that he merely notices Fabius Maximus Cunctātor. In reading, observe the *féssurrápitis*, the low pitch on *ī* in fábiī, (where we English use a high pitch,) the emphasis on *tū*, the treatment of *Máximus* as a name, as there had been several of that name, but he was the only one, *ūnus* (keep the *us* long) who by such an act as *cunctándō* (which should be very significantly spoken as quite contrary to Roman *élan*) would save the state (*rē*). The *quīnōbis* should be long and even, as the voice must be prepared for the *cunctándō*, before which it is best to take breath. The

two last words form the difficulty. The rhythm has
been already alluded to in Art. 50. The *res* must be
quite long, and low, but strong; the *sti* high and short,
descending rapidly to the *ēs*, when, the voice unexpectedly
and unusually rises in *rê*, only to fall again in the same
syllable.

The last seven lines are a kind of Roman anticipation
of " Rule Britannia ! " They must have been repeated
over and over again with extreme unction[1] by warlike
political Romans, who despised the versatile scientific
Greek. They contain the glorification of a system of
repression, conquest and government, as opposed to all
that was lofty in art and science, and they must be
spoken as if the speaker fully entered into the sentiment.
The *álii* are of course the Greeks, whom Anchīses does
not even deign to name. This word *álii* must have a
chief emphasis, which can be principally produced by
lengthening and reinforcing the final *i*, and as this is
quite opposed to our English *ē·liąi,* it will require care.
The opposition to *álii* is *tū*, which must be brought out
with great emphasis, and breath should be taken after
it. The other important words are *hâè* and *ártēs* in (8).
The tone of the first lines is given by the *crēdoéquidē* (4);
—" of course, who disputes it? but what matter? be it
so, they are smarter and 'cuter, but—*we* can thrash
'em ! " Hence lines (3) to (6) have to be spoken in a
sort of depreciatory high and hollow tone. At the same
time great care must be taken with the opening molossī,
(excū'dent, ōrā'bunt, dēscrī'bent). In beginning (7) the
tone of voice changes, and becomes round, solemn and
assertive ; *tû*—" this is what you have to," (take breath

---

[1] In anything but the Roman Catholic sense of the words.

here,) *régereimpériō pópulōs.* The high-pitched syllables are all short, the whole force of the sentence depends on the length and delivery of the three long syllables *im, ō, ōs.* The last words of the line are light, because they are so obvious that the listener supplies them at once, though they are still solemn, as befits an injunction. Fancy how a whole forum of Romans would rise at the words, and speak them with their feeling. Then comes, "*these* are to be *your* arts," in English the "*your*" would be emphasised, and considerable meaning would be thrown into the long but unemphatic *arts.* In Latin the dissyllable *ártēs* supplies the place of both English syllables. The strong *tú* in the preceding line, renders *tíbi* weak, and allows it to be slurred on to *érunt,* so that the whole force falls on *ártēs,*—"these are your substitutes for the arts, you are *governors, men* (virī) not mechanics (hominēs)." Then the idea is further developed, and the three special arts alluded to are described : to impose your own laws upon others, to *spare* (we know how Romans spared) those that submit, and—to put your heel on those who resist. This is the spirit to be infused into the utterance. The effect is obtained by the pronunciation of *impṓnere,* with very long *im,* and steady, decided, unhurried, but very emphatic *pṓnere;* by making *párcere* quiet, but with a kind of tone, implying,—"oh yes ! of course, we spare them,"—and throwing the chief force on *subjéctīs,* where *sub* must be long, and the rise and fall of pitch with the length of the *tīs* be so managed as to give the feeling—"yes, if they give up everything and surrender unconditionally ; " and then, gathering strength on the three following long and low syllables *etdḗbel,* rise with a kind of quiet exultation on *lâ* and finish by bringing out the *pér* in *supérbōs* with a savage emphasis which shews that every one who ventures to oppose Rome has a proud spirit which *must* and *shall* be humbled.

It is very difficult to describe these points in language at all, and hence the schoolboy slang which I have used must be forgiven. The reader must endeavour to realise them by repeating these wonderful lines till they are perfectly familiar to him, and he will have then learned more of Latin pitch-accent and quantity, with freedom of force, and the great variety of oratorical power which this allows, than by any other means that I know.

ART. 123. *Example C.*—The story of these lines is well known. M. Claudius C. f. C. n. Marcellus, the hope of Augustus and the Romans had died (B.C. 23) the year before they were written, in his twentieth year. All Rome had flocked to his funeral, and Augustus himself had pronounced the funeral oration.

Aenēās sees the shade of this youth accompanying the great M. Claudius M. f. M. n. Marcellus (B.C. 268—208) :—

> Atque hīc Aenēās, ūnā namque īre vidēbat
> ēgregium formā juvenem et fulgentibus armīs,
> sed frons laeta parum, et dējectō lumina vultū :
> Quis, pater, ille virum quī sīc comitātur euntem?
> Fīlius, anne aliquis magnā dē stirpe nepōtum ?
> Quī strepitus circā comitum ! quantum instar in ipsō !
> Sed nox ātra caput tristī circumvolat umbrā.
> tum pater Anchīsēs, lacrymīs ingressus obortīs :—

and answers in the words of (C.).

These lines, recited by Virgil himself to Augustus and his sister Octāvia, the mother of Marcellus, must have

H

been, in the poet's eyes, the best that he could make,
and are therefore extremely well adapted for an exercise
in Latin rhythm.   It so happens also that they exem-
plify the treatment of the final *m* in a most remarkable
manner, and have been re-written for that purpose in
Art. 97.   Only a few hints need be added.

   Line (1) is mere sadness.   Line (2) depends for its
force on *osténdent* and *tántum,* and its great accumulation
of spondees.   Lines (3) and (4) are a passionate appeal
to the gods, and at the same time an outrageous flattery
of the Romans.   The chief words are *nímium* (3) and
háèc (4).   Lines (5) to (7) are reminiscences of the
mighty pageant of the funeral, the chief words are *quántōs, vírūm, quáè,* and the melancholy *recéntem,* which,
scarcely in character where it stands, spoke volumes to
Augustus and Octāvia.   Then comes a more cheerful,
though regretful view of Marcellus's prowess.   Take
care of *Íliacā,* on account of the fearful English *ilai·acə.*
The *quísquaddégénte, intántusspè, ullō* are the important
points.   Then comes the exclamation of regret for losing
one that shewed such eminent filial affection (pietās),
bringing back the days of " old faith," (just as the
German prides himself on *alte deutsche Treue,*) and then
such wonderful success in war as his youthful feats would
lead one to hope.   It is on the last of course that most
stress is laid.   Observe that *pietās* and *fidēs* will acquire
their chief effect from their final long syllables with a
low pitch, the descent of the voice allowing of great expression of regret, and the long quantities of the vowels
giving abundant opportunity of developing it.   Observe
especially *invictáque* (11) with the high pitch transferred
to the short vowel *á* to mark the enclitic addition.   The

contrast in (13, 14) is between *pédes* and *équī*, but after *armā'tō* the two lines may be spoken rapidly.

The next line (15) begins with quite a new strain, as mournful and tender as possible. *Miseránde,* must be well brought out, and the two first syllables must *not* be those in the English *miserable,* but clear *mi-se-.* *Púer* may occasion some difficulty, but great tenderness can be conveyed by the fall of the voice, and the lengthened second syllable. In *quâ* the greatest stress is reached, the following *fâtaáspera rúmpās,* are tearful, broken voiced, but quiet. Then in (16) we have the soft penetrating *tû marcéllus éris,* on hearing which Octāvia fainted, so that probably Virgil never finished his recitation. But I recommend the whole of the rest of the speech to be finished in a low, weak, rather hurried, mournful tone, till it dies off at *mū'nere.* The assimilated *m* in (17) and the slur in (18) must be carefully studied and steadily attacked, and the final *ī* in *inā'nī* must have its full effect, for though the tone is that of a man who has lost all heart, yet as the reader is a totally different person, he must be particularly careful not to make the speech ridiculous by ludicrous errors of pronunciation.

ART. 124. *Example D.*—In (D.) the whole character of the verse is changed. We have still hexameters certainly, but they have no roll, they are verses of society, charming by the way in which they set colloquialisms to metre. The present passage has been selected for its variety in a short space, and the great numbers of spondees it contains.

Begin with a quiet interrogative tone, pausing in (1) at *fīt, maccé'nās,* and *nēmō,* emphasising *quássibi* distinctly, and in (2) bringing out the two *seu* and contrasting the *rátiō* and *fors* (beware of final *z*). The *rátiō* and *déderit* will derive their chief force from their long final syllables. After *objĕ́cerit* pause again, and then take *íllā*, making the double *l* quite distinct, and the *ā* long with the descending pitch.   All three lines are to be spoken in a tone of amused argumentative puzzlement.

In (4) the old soldier speaks, and the words must be in a tone of longing envy, to which the words of four long syllables, with a final low pitch, and very long vowels, add great force. At *grávis ánnīs* change the tone to Horace's, who says, "there you see, this is why he says it."   The *grávis* must be short (beware of English *grḗvis*), and the double *n* and long *ī* of *ánnīs* must make a strong contrast (beware of reducing the word to English *anise*).   In (6) the words introduce the merchant, with a parenthetical explanation of his opinion,— "you know, his ships were in a storm at the time,"— which shews how to bring out the *nā'vījac-*, all the syllables quite long.   In (7, 8) we have the merchant's speech. Beware of calling *mīlítia* like the English *milish'ə*.   The *quídenī* for *quid enim*, had possibly only one syllable with raised pitch.   Many instances of *enim, quidem, autem,* seem to me to come under Quintilian's rule of junctūra. But begin *ccon-* with energetic *c*.   In (8) we have the difficulty of two long syllables being slurred *mōméntō aut,* and there must be a pause between them, see Art. 58, *c*. For such verses the ear will sufficiently recognise the intention even if neither of them is much shortened. Be very particular with the pyrrhics *cíta, vénit,* in (8).

In (9) mind the *ag-* to lengthen the first syllable, and the two assimilated *m*.   In (10), the *subgállī cántū* must be spoken with a tone which shews that it was only the unconscionably early hour of rousing which could have led the lawyer to such an opinion. The slur in *consúltorúbióstia púlsat* will require some practice to execute neatly. Say *ós-ti-a*, not *óstja*. In (11) bring out the *ílle* (with distinct double *l*) as referring to the *consúltor* who is an *agrícola*. The *dátīs rádibus*, being so different from the common English *dē·tis vē·dibəs*, will require care to preserve the high initial pitch and the final long syllables. In (12) much effect can be produced by the wondering longing tone of the farmer's first three words.

Then in (13) everything is changed. The tone becomes quick and petulant, the parenthetical *ádɛō sunt múlta*, shews that Horace is tired of enumerating cases which would tire even gossiping Fabiús. The long *ō* in *ádeō* allows of much effect in the tone. In (14), *nê tê·mórer* is quick, and the last word very rapid. Observe the *m*'s in *quô rêddēdū'cā* in (15), and particularly the *ên égo* as distinct from our common English *en ī·gō'*. In (16) the assimilated *m* is important, *jáffáciacquíd vóltis*. All this speech of the god (15 to 19) should be read in a quiet ordering tone, but very carefully as to quantities. Line (17) requires great care, as well as *mutātīs* in (18). For *ēja! stātis?* (19), see Art. 115. The *nō'lint* (19) belongs to Horace, with an amused tone implying, "they wouldn't, I told you so." Then comes the remark on their refusing happiness when in their power.

The last three lines are in an indignantly contemptuous, though still almost conversational tone. The *méritō* is the chief word, and owes its weight to the final long syllable. Take breath after *jū'piter*. The whole three lines are in close connection and in one characteristic quality of tone.

ART. 125. *Example E.*—We now come to a totally
different style of poetry. In lyrics the metrical rhythm
must be always well brought out, but in general with
very little chant. The (E., F., I., K.) have totally different characters, and the chant belongs to (I.) only.
Each ode of Horace indeed requires a distinct study.
(E., F.) are given for the sake of the choriambs. In
(E.) there are two in each line, and the first ends a word,
but there is a spondee at the beginning connected with
the first, which must be well brought out, and an iamb
or pyrrhic at the end connected with the last, so that
there is in many lines a false appearance of ending
with two dactyles. Many lines are read by English boys
as if they had three final dactyles, thus :—

misī nǝs at·ǝvis ed·iti redj·ibǝs,

using *dj* for English *j*. All that is absolutely absurd.
To bring out the choriambs nicely, the last long syllable
of the second should be slightly lengthened, and the
voice should grow weaker for an instant before proceeding to the next syllable, but care should be taken not
absolutely to divide the last word into two. This may be
indicated by a hyphen before the | which separates the
feet ; thus :—

maecē'- | nās átavīs | ē'dite rē'- | gibus.

Line (2) will require considerable care to bring out
the slur properly, and so will (7). There must be a
slight pause after the second *et* in (2) and this gives an
opportunity for a slight "gush" on *dúlce*.

In (3) put an emphasis on *quôs*,—"*some* like to do
this," together with many other things in the lines omitted,

—as opposed to the *mê* of lines (7) and (8). Be careful to indicate the raised pitch in *mētáque* (4), *palmáque* (5), see p. 29, note 1. In (6), the contrast of *terrā'ruddóminōs* and *děōs* led me accidentally, when I was reading the lines out, to raise my pitch on the last syllable of *děōs*, and, though I immediately corrected the error, I mention it to shew the difficulty of overcoming national habits. It would be equally wrong to raise the pitch of the voice on *ad*, and that creates the difficulty. Read :—

> terrā' | ruddóminōs | ē'vehit ad- | děōs

and mark the contrast between the two first words and the last by the quality of tone used for the final long *ōs* in *děōs*.

In (7) be careful of *t* in frón- | tium, and in (8) and (9) mind the three assimilated *m*'s. In (10) be careful of *tī'biās*, which as an English word we call *tib·iəz*. Also remember the initial spondee, and the assimilated *m* in (12), producing the slight lengthening just mentioned, and the double *r*, as lesbō'- | urréfugit | .

Great effect can be given to the two last lines, which close the dedication. The sentiment is, "I am satisfied with all this, and have no such desires of athletic honours, or political office, or wealth or hunting &c. as I have mentioned; but—if only—you—will place me among—*lyric*—poets, I shall be as proud as a god." Make short pauses after *quod—sī—mê*—come with a joyous "gush" upon *ly'riās*, lengthening out the last syllable, and getting immense expression out of the fall of pitch from the short high pitch of the first syllable. In (14) *sub-lī-* | *mī* there must be a slight echo of the commencement of the preceding line. Then fériās- |

sī'dera vér- | tice, first falls down quickly to a slight pause without separation, (of the kind already mentioned) and the voice rises again to a magnificent *sī'dera*, the last word being comparatively unimportant.

ART. 126. *Example F.*—Here there are three choriambs, the first and last are treated as in E., the middle one is always quite distinct, as, scīrenéfās, Leucónoē, útmélius; séutrĭbuit, dēbĭlitat, vînalíquēs, dúllóquimur, quámmĭnimū, and are seen to be much varied in pitch-accent.

Suppose Horace to be sitting one winter's night before his table with a bowl of Falernian, while on the other side pretty Leuconoe is " telling fortunes " with " Babylonian numbers " and other contrivances. Horace looks at her amused for some time, and then bursts out with, " Don't look how long we've to live, Leuconoe, it's not right! and don't try your Babylonian contrivances. How much better it is to endure whatever happens (with stoic dignity), whether we are to live long or die now. Be wise my girl, and drink, (like an epicūrī dē grege porcus !) and for the short present renounce the long future. Don't you see, time is flying while we speak ; make use of *now* and a fig for *then!*" This, in purposely unpoetical language, seems the gist of the original. On this view lines (1) to (3) are a kind of paternal rebuke, in a pleasant tone of voice, however, half coaxing. But when the stoic comes out, the voice and manner change almost to that of (K.), the *útmélius*, *quícquid érit*, and especially the *pátī* (where the descent of tone and final long syllable are capable of great effect)* must be strongly brought out. The next two lines to the beginning of (6), and especially all (5), which is wonderfully, of course purposely, monotonous, may be rapid, but take breath after *máre*, in order to run on quickly from *tyrrhē'num* on to a loud, bold, commanding and yet jovial *sápiās*, with an assimilated *m*, as tyrrhē'- | nussápiās | , then the *vînalíquēs* is quite in the jolly manner, which is continued in the following words, where *brévi* must be well emphasised, and in running on spêllón- | garrésecēs | , the last word must come out very strong and decided, with the chief force and highest pitch on *ré* (which must be kept short), and then without running on to *s*, the energy of speech must expend itself on the low *cēs* (keep *c*, *s* as pure *k*, *s*). Then make a pause and resume in quite an altered quiet tone, dúllóquimur | fū'gerit ín- | vida | ae'tās | and then encouragingly cár- pediē |, and with an implied smiling shake of the head : cquámmínimū | ccrē'dula póst- | erō.

ART. 127. *Example G.*—This and (H.) are introduced for the sake of the choriambic pentameters. Observe in (G.) the strictly choriambic terminations *mīlítiae* (2), *carmínibus* (4), *indómínū* (6), with a pitch-accent rhythm quite different from Ovid's, which is only found in (8). The piece is not particularly good for declamation, but the flattery of (3), with the attestation *ita sĭffē'lĭx*, and the parenthetical good wishes of (4) admit of a little variety, as also the parenthetical *utconsvē'mus* (5). The assimilated final *m* must be observed in (6) and (7), and care must be taken to preserve *in* long in (7) and *ge* short, as : nectántuingíniō quántusservîre dolō'rī.

ART. 128. *Example H.*—This is a sample of those monotonous Ovidian "longs and shorts" which so afflicted our school life. It is necessary thoroughly to understand the cadence of the final choriambs : ípsevéní

(2), trôjafúit (4), a | dúlter áquīs (6), re | lícta díēs (8), têla mánūs (10), which ought not now to occasion any difficulty. Their monotony of pitch-accent is wonderful. Be careful of the *m* in (5). Take breath after *desérto* and *quaeréntī* (9) in order to run on *jacuísseffrīgida* (7), and *spatiō'saffállere* (9), making the *sef, saf* quite long, but entirely without emphasis and in low pitch.

ART. 129. *Example I.*—Sapphics put on very different characters in Horace's odes. The present example is devotional and was meant to be sung or chanted. It will be advisable to put a little chant into it therefore. These stanzas are chosen because they give three instances (1, 9, 10) of a break in the line opposed to English habits. Chant then solemnly, and bring out the choriamb distinctly, thus :—

> phóèbe sylvā- | rúcque pótens | diā'na,
> lū'ciduccoe-' | lī décus, ô | coléndī
> sémper et cúl- | tī, dáte quáè | precā'mur
> témpore sác- | rō.

Be careful with assimilated *m* in (7, 9) and especially (10), the last is

> spêbbónaccer- | tácque dómur- | repórtō

and breath should be taken after *que.* See p. 74, note.

ART. 130. *Example K.*—This is completely stoical, lauding the immovability of the "just" man. It is therefore a bold piece of declamation. There must be a pause after *et* (1), the slur in (2), *nôn cī'vi-uár-dor,* requires especial practice to save it from *nôn cī'vju-árdor,* with an *hiātus* : but *nôn cī'vi wárdor* would be preferable to this. Practice *uárdor* separately, and *cī'viu* separately, and then put them together. Bring out the molossus *instántis* in (3). The *méntequátit | sólidā |* must be bold and fine ; the effect depends, as so often before, on the length and low pitch of the last syllables. In (6) make a point of *fulminántis*, and run *mágnajóvis* into a distinct choriamb. But reserve force for (7) and (8). There must be quiet preparation first for the explosion on *bā* (7) after the long syllables *illā*, and for the strong *impávidufférient*, where the effect is produced by the long but low pitched *im* and *duf*. The *ruīnae* is a comparatively quiet word because its coming has been so thoroughly anticipated.

ART. 131. *Example L.*—This is a piece of fun throughout, which is explained by the last four lines. An old usurer is seized with a false sentiment for country life, and gloats over what he fancies would be its amusements to him, but which of course would prove dreadful annoyances to a man who had lived such a life as his. So he works himself up through some 66 lines of false sentiment, of which oñly 18 are given in (L.), into a determination to give up his usury and go to the country. Whereupon he. calls in all his capital in the middle of the month, and at the end of a fortnight he is so disgusted with his venture that he tries to reinvest the whole. This false sentiment is easy to express, and no harm is done if it is ludicrously exaggerated. Hence the first four lines can be spoken with a wonderful variety of pitch, the high tones rising to a kind of falsetto. In *prócul* (1) lengthen the *cul* greatly, and similarly the final *ís* in *negó'tiīs*. Mind the spondee in (2), contrast the *patérna* and *suīs*, and bring out the molossus (*exércet*) in (3), and in (4) mind the long *nī* of *ómnī*, of which much may be made in expression. Line (17) will require care on account of its trissyllabic measures and final *m.* At (19) the voice and manner entirely changes. The writer gives the key to the mystery and dismisses the usurer caustically. Pay attention to the mental effect of *jamjam,* as well as to its phonetic effect of assimilated *m,* as *já'ijaffutū'rus rū'sticus,* (p. 66, note 2) and mind the spondee in the third place. In (21) attend both to mental and phonetic effect of *ómnerredêgit.* After this line pause, and give the last line in a quiet cutting tone. See also the remarks on p. 77.

XIII. How to Read the Prose Examples in the Appendix.

ART. 132. These cannot be considered in such detail, for I despair of making myself intelligible except by reading the passages. But I will observe upon necessarily unemphatic words, such as, *autem, etiam, quidem, enim,* &c., and the probability that they also came under Quintilian's rule of junctūrae. Thus in (M. 1), *éstáutein* or *éstautein* will come in weakly, and lead up to the molossus *dĭcĕud̄o* which must be clear and decided, while *étiā* will fall weak. Then *equădaccántus* will be distinct and important, and *obscū'rior* must end with a clear dactyle. Difficulties arise in long words with several long and short syllables mixed in a manner which could scarcely occur in verse, except rarely in lyrics, as ōrātiōnē (M. 4), modulārêtur (M. 4), ad áuriūvoluptā'tessequâtur indústria (M. 6), multitū'dō (N. 2), longitū'dinuet brevitā'tuīnsónis (N. 4, 5), animadvérsiō (O. 6), nōminántur (N. 9), jūdíciussuperbíssimu (Q. 6). It is only by studying such separate little phrases that these difficulties can be overcome. It is principally necessary to keep the quantities pure, but care must also be taken to raise and lower the pitch of the voice in the right places.

Art. 133.—*Example M.* offers no difficulties beyond what have been mentioned. It is a quiet piece of lecture delivery in which every point should be neatly and cleanly rendered without fuss or mouthing.

Art. 134. *Example N.* is similar, but (1, 2) relate a fact, which has to be emphasised by *tôta* and *ū'nā sy'llabā*, while (2) and (3) states another fact, advanced in a different tone of voice, and (4) to (6) gives Cicero's explanation of both, and all this should be indicated by the character of tone employed.

Art. 135.—*Example O.* is also a lecture piece, but (12) and (13) are capable of a little point, by funnily emphasising the *cōmicō'rum* and especially the *abjĕctī*.

Art. 136.—*Example P.* is a criticism on the rhythmical character of a sentence. Only the last word of the first clause is here given, but it should be read as a de- . clamatory terminal, "persolu'tās," with much orotundity. Then comes parenthically the name of the foot (*dīchorēus*), in a quiet explanatory tone of voice, followed by remarks (one taken from another section of the book), on the indifferent quantity of final syllables. Afterwards another sentence is taken, which must be delivered with great orotundity, as if at a public assembly, to bring out the final *dīchorēus*, which, in a perfectly quiet altered tone, must be stated to have had such an "admirable" effect. Then a query : " Did this depend on the sense or the rhythm ? Try. Change the order." Then the order is changed and the reader should endeavour to make the

final paeon *teméritās* as effective as possible, in order to
bring out the justness of the following criticism, *jánni-
hilérit /* said in a quiet rather high off-hand tone, such as
is often adopted in similar circumstances on the Continent. The disagreement from Aristotle (see Cicero's
original bowing to his author, quia optimus autor ita
censet, in Art. 109) must be given with some unction,
and the last sentence must be well contrasted and emphasised.   Observe : at éadeu·vér·ba, éades·sentén·tia,
ánimō·ístūc sátisést·, áu·ribus nôn·sátis.   The last
dactyle must come out well, and we must feel that
it is preceded by a cretic.   The nature of the feet
in the *cadence* of all clauses (not merely of sentences)
were, if we may trust their expressions, always brought
out by Cicero and Quintilian.

ART. 137.—*Example Q.* contains extremely important
remarks on slurred and gaping vowels, but is all in the
quiet critical style.   With this we may compare Quintilian : dīlūcida vērō erit prōnuntiātiō [delivery] prīmum,
sī verba tōta ēxierint, quōrum pars dīvorārē, pars dēstituī
solet, plērīsque ēxtrēmās syllabās nōn perferentibus, dum
priōrum sonō indúlgent, [shewing Latin vicious habits,
comparable to our own, and explaining many subsequent
changes.]   Ut est autem necessāria verbōrum ēxplānātiō
[clear utterance ;] ita omnēs imputāre·et velut annume-
rāre litterās molestum et ōdiōsum, [which must be particularly noted, but foreigners are always allowed to
speak with more distinctness than natives, without being
stigmatised as molestī et ōdiōsī, thus Gaelic and Welsh
English is often felt to be "prettier" and "pleasanter"
than our own more freely treated language.]   Nam et
vōcālēs frequentissimē coeunt [slur into one another,] et

consonantium quaedam [he is evidently thinking principally of *m* but he is allowing for old *s* and other examples in Cic. *Or.* §§ 153—162] īnsequente vōcālī dissimulātur ["made to appear something else," this is its literal meaning, but in White's Latin Dictionary it is in this passage translated by a totally different metaphor as "absorbed." Observe how this interpretation supports that given to *in eam transīre* on p. 60.] Utrique exemplum posúimus : *multum ille et terrīs.* Vītātur etiam duriōrum inter sē congréssus, unde *pellexit* et *collégit*, &c. (11, 3, 33—35).

ART. 138. *Example R.*—The story of Gracchus's piper is here told as a dialogue and allows of a little, not much, alteration of voice. The parenthesis (3-5) should be marked, for the connection of Gracchus with cum eburneolā solitus est habēre fistulā quī stāret &c. (3, 5) is not very clear to an Englishman, and will require some management of the voice to bring out. Observe cuccontiōnārētur (6). The observation of Catulus (9, 10) must be made in quite another tone of voice. Then Crassus returns and begins meditating on Gracchus's treason—and I have taken advantage of Julius's cutting him short to cut him still shorter. The *mitte óbsecrō*, is a polite stop, and the last words of Julius's speech, cūjus ego nōndum &c. admit of considerable expression as shewing that he had failed to understand the reason. Now whether the reason given by Crassus is right or wrong it is not very possible to say. I must own I am not satisfied with it, and I think Quintilian's version more likely to be correct, judging from Cicero's further account of the extremely artificial character of Gracchus's oratory :—

Quid fuit in Gracchō? quem tū, Catule, melius meministī, quod
mē [Cotta is speaking] puerō tantopere ierrētur [C. Gracchus was
killed B.C. 122, Cotta was born B.C. 124.]   "Quō mē miser con-
feram? quō vertam? in Capitōliumne? at frātris sanguine redundat :
an domum? mātremne ut miseram lāmentantemque videam, et abjec-
tam?"   Quae sīc ab illō acta [delivered, not 'acted'] esse constābat,
oculīs, vōce, gestū, inimīcī ut lacrimās tenēre non possent.   Haec
eō dīcō plūribus, quod genus hōc tōtum ōrātorēs, quī sunt vēritātis
ipsīus actōrēs, relīquērunt; imitātōrēs autem vēritātis histriōnēs
occupāvērunt. (CIC. *De Or.* book iii. § 214.)

It is evident that the whole manner of Gracchus had
become traditional, even in Cicero's time, and that therefore Crassus's explanation can only be a theory.

Now Quintilian was of course still farther off, and
possibly he took the tale from Cicero whom he is continually quoting, but, speaking of the relation of oratory
to music he says

UUnō interim contentī sīmus exemplō C. Gracchī, praecipuī
suōrum temporum ōrātōris, cui contiōnantī consistens post eum
mūsicus fiṣtulā, quam tonarion [pitch pipe] vocant, modōs, quibus
dēbēret intendī, monstrābat.   Haec eī cūra inter turbidissimās
actiōnes vel terrentī optimātēs vel jam timentī prōfuit (1, 10,
27).   *more useful*

Now the "modōs" would seem to imply the *cadences*
which were peculiar to the Greek musical modes, and it
appears to me, that, although very possibly Quintilian
used the word at a venture knowing little of musical
theory, this is a more likely solution than Cicero's, put
into the mouth of Crassus, since these different "musical
modes" were especially suitable to Gracchus's theatrical
oratory.

At the end of Crassus's explanation, the last lines of
advice may be given in a quiet little preceptorial manner,

" of course you will understand that the piper is to be left at home, and only the meaning of his piping brought with you to the forum."

ART. 139.—*Example S.* is Italian and not Latin at all, but I attempted to recite it when reading my paper, in order to shew the precise nature of the phonetic facts on which I have founded the explanation of slurred vowels, and omitted but assimilated *m*. It is retained here in order that the reader may be able to verify these facts, by getting Italian natives who have had a literary education and speak pure Tuscan, to read the passage to him, so that he may really hear and understand for himself that these theories are founded on living realities.

XIV. Conclusion.

ART. 140.—Notwithstanding the theoretical points which have been touched upon in the arguments raised in favour of the method for the treatment of slurred vowels and final M, here proposed, of which the latter forms the greatest novelty in this tract, yet I hope that I have not belied the promise of my title and of my opening paragraph, but have furnished strictly practical rules for arriving at a feeling for ancient Roman rhythm in verse and in prose, quantitative and accentual. It is perhaps scarcely necessary to observe that even if my theory of assimilated *m* be not accepted, through the great prejudice in favour of the use of pure final *m*, dating from the time when Latin, having broken up into separate languages for common use, was restudied as

I

a dead language with modern usages, and without a consciousness of the ancient treatment, to which the modern
form of the derived languages was obviously due,—yet
even if *m* be retained, if Quintilian's lament (in him
certainly quite alphabetical) over the frequency of the
" lowing " final *m* be justified by scholastic usage, all the
rest of the work that I have done is as available as ever
for practical use, and will equally well serve to give
a feeling for the rhythm of Latin speech which is of
course dependent principally on a strict observance of
the laws of length and pitch, and independent to a great
extent of particular alphabetic usages. But allow me
finally to draw attention to the absolute necessity of
general phonologic studies to all those who would deal
with the intricate questions of classical pronunciation,
not merely Latin, which is comparatively easy, although
very very far from having been completely investigated,
but especially Greek, which presents problems of remarkable difficulty. Those who have hitherto written on
the subject have seldom known much more of phonology
than they could learn by speaking their own language,
without thinking of how they spoke, or of what speech was.
But for such investigations as the present, an acquaint-
ance with the habits of many nations is indispensable,
and of the historical alteration of sounds. It will have
been seen that I was led to my theory of final M by
delicate observations on the synthesis of Italian sounds,
scarcely known, and seldom even mentioned in Italian
books, which I owe entirely to Prince Louis Lucien
Bonaparte. It is also necessary to become acquainted
with the phonetic facts which have underlain explanations
by grammarians who were but roughly acquainted with

their nature, in order to have a glimpse of the meaning of
other grammarians who are presenting unknown facts. If
I have in any way succeeded in putting together a "work-
ing model" of Augustan speech,—with of course all the
roughness and incompleteness of a model,—I owe my
success to my previous phonologic studies for more than
thirty years, and to my yet unfinished historical studies
during the last ten years, on Early and Existing English
Pronunciation, received and dialectal.

APPENDIX

OF

QUANTITATIVE EXAMPLES.

Note.— *The diphthongs* ae, oe, au, eu, ui, *being naturally long, are unmarked. Other naturally long vowels are marked* ā, ē, ī, ō, ū. *Short vowels are left unmarked. The consonant which " makes position" is followed by a hyphen, as in* ip-se.—Art. 22. 30.

Vowels connected by ‿ *are to be slurred together in one syllable, this mark is not used in the prose examples.*—Art. 58. ·

In example A only, a high pitch of voice sustained throughout an entire syllable is marked by an acute accent, as ómnēs ; *when the pitch of the voice rises and falls again in the same syllable the circumflex accent is used, as* ô-ra. *Unaccented vowels are in a lower pitch of voice. The acute accent is retained before* que *in all the examples, as* metáque.—Art 41.

A small m *as in* quan-quam‿animus *is to be entirely neglected. An* m- *at the end of words, or in* m-que, *making "position" as* jam-nox, certám-que *is not to be sounded at all, but is to be made effective by pronouncing the following consonant as if it were double, thus* jánnóx certácque, *or by lengthening the preceding vowel before a pause, as,* dolō′rē.—Art. 91.

The numbers following the title of any example, refer to the pages on which that example is cited, and an asterisk indicates the page where special explanations are given. See generally, Arts. 115 —139.

Example S. is Italian, not Latin, and illustrates slurred vowels and unwritten consonants assimilated in speech, not quantity.

A.

Aenēas's Introduction to his Account of the Destruction of Troy.

See pp. 32. 33. 37. 40. 41. 42. 67. 68. 90*.

con-ticuêre̱ óm-nēs, in-teu-tîque̱ ôra tene̓'han-t.

2 ín-de tórō páter aenē'ās- sîc ór-sus ab ál-tō :
    īn-fán-duḿ-, rēgîna, júbēs- renovâre dolō'rem-,'

4 trōjā́nās ut ópēs et- lāmen-tā'bile rég-nu^m
    ērúerin-t dánaī, quaeque̱ íp-se misér-rima vī'dī,

6 et- quō'rum- pár-s mág-na fúī.   quís- tā'lia fán-dō
    myr-mídonum- dolopúm-ve̱ aut- dū'rī mîles ulíx-ī

8 tém-peret ā lácrymīs? et- jám- nóx- hū'mida coe'lō
    praecípitat-, svādén-tque cadén-tia sī'dera sóm-nōs-.

10 sed-, sī tán-tus ámor- cā'sūs- cognós-cere nō's-trōs
    et- bréviter- trō'jae sup-rē'mu^m audī're labō'rem-,—

12 quán-qua^m ánimus- meminís-se̱ hór-ret- lūc-tū'que refûgi:
    in-cípiam-.   frác-tī bél-lō fātī's-que repúl-sī

14 duc-tō'rēs- dánaūm-, tót- jám- lābén-tibus án-ṇīs
    ī'n-star- món-tis équum- (dīvī'nā- pál-ladis ár-te

16 aedífican-t, sec-tā'que̱ in-téx-un-t áb-jete cós-tās ;
    võ'tum- prō réditū símulan-t ; éa fâma vagâtur.

18 hûc dēléc-ta vírūm- sor-tī'tī cór-pora fū'r-ti^m /
    in-clū'dun-t cae'cō láterī, penitús-que cavér-nās

20 ingén-tēs uterúm-que̱ ar-mā'tō mī'lite cóm-plen-t.
    és-t in con-spéc-tū ténedos-, nōtís-sima fā'mā

22 ī'n-sula, dîves ópum-, príamī dum- rég-na mane̓'ban-t,
    núnc tan-tum- siṇús et- státiō malefîda carī'nīs ;

24 hûc sê prōvéc-tī dēsér-tō in lī'tore cón-dun-t ;
    nôs abiís-se rátī, et- vén-tō petiís-se mycē'nās.

VIRG. *Aen.* ii. 1—25.

B.

Roman Policy as contrasted with Greek Art.

See pp. 32. 33. 34. 40. 41. 68. 94*.

quō fes-sum- rapitis-, fabiī? ṭū max-imus il-le̱ ēs,

2 ūnús- quī ṇōbīs- cun-ctan-dō res-tituēs- rē^m.

ex-cūden-t aliī spīran-tia mol-lius aera,
4   crēdo‿equidem-; vīvōs- dūcen-t dē mar-more vul-tūs,
    ō‚ābun-t causās- melius-, coelī'que meātūs-
6   dēscrīben-t radiō‿et- sur-gen-tia sīdera dīcen-t ;
    tū regere‿im-periō populōs-, rōmāne, memen-tō :
8   hae tibi‿erun-t ar-tēs-, pācīs-que‿im-pōnere mōrem- ;
    par-cere sub-jec-tīs, et- dēbel-lāre super-bōs.

                                        VIRG. *Aen.* vi. 845—853.

C.

Lament for Marcellus.

See pp. 32. 33. 41. 71*. 97*.

ō nāte‿in-gen-tem- lūc-tum- nē quaere tuōruᵐ.
2   os-ten-den-t ter-rīs hun-c tan-tum- fāta, neque‿ultrā
    es-se sinen-t.   nimium- vōbīs- rōmāna propāgō
4   vīsa poten-s, superī, propria‿haec- sī dōna fuis-sen-t.
    quan-tōs il-le virūm- mag-nam- māvor-tis ad ur-bem-
6   cam-pus aget- gemitūs- ; vel- quae, tiberīne, vidēbis-
    fūnera, quum- tumulum- praeter-lābēre recen-tem- !
8   nec puer īliacā quis-quam- dē gen-te latīnōs
    in- tan-tum- spē tol-let avōs-, nec- rōmula quon-daᵐ
10 ul-lō sē tan-tum- tel-lūs jac-tābit alum-nō.
    heu pietās, heu pris-ca fidēs, in-vic-táque bel-lō
12 dex-tera ! nōn il-lī sē quis-quaᵐ‿im-pūne tulis-set
    ob-vius armātō, seu quum- pedes īret in hos-tem‿
14 seu spūman-tis equī foderet- cal-cāribus ar-mōs.
    heu, miseran-de puer-, sī quā fāta‿as-pera rum-pās
16 tū mar-cel-lus eris-.   manibus- date līlia plēnīs- ;
    pur-pureōs- spar-gam- flōrēs, animám-que nepōtis
18 hīs sal-teᵐ‿ac-cumulem- dōnīs, et- fun-gar inānī
    mūnere.   VIRG. *Aen.* vi. 868—886,

D.

No One Contented with his Lot.

See pp. 17. 32. 33. 40. 68. 99*.

    quī fīt-, maecēnās, ut- nēmō, quam- sibi sor-tem-
2 seu ratiō dederit-, seu for-s ob-jēcerit, il-lā
    con-fĕn-tus- vīvat-, laudet- dīver-sa sequen-tēs?
4 "ō for-tūnātī mer-cātōrēs!" grăvis an-nīs
    mīles ait-, mul-tō jam- frac-tus- mem-bra labōre.
6 con-trā mer-cātor-, nāvim- jac-tan-tibus austrīs :
    "mīlitia es-t potior-.   quid enim-? con-cur-ritur ; hōrae
8 mōmen-tō aut cită mor-s venĭt, aut vīc-tōria laeta."
    ag-ricolam- laudat- jūris- lēgúm-que perītus-,
10 sub- gal-lī cantum- con-sul-tor ubi os-tia pul-sat.
    il-le, datīs- vadibus- quī rūre ex-trac-tus in ur-bem es-t,
12 sōlōs- fēlīcēs- vīven-tēs- clāmat in ur-be.
    cētera dē genere hōc, adeō sun-t mul-ta, loquācem-
14 dēlas-sāre valen-t fabium-.   nē tē morer, audī,
    quō rēm- dēdūcam-. sī quis- deus, "ēn ego," dīcat,
16 "jam- faciam- quid- vol-tis ; eris- tū, quī modo mīles-,
    mer-cātor-; tū, con-sul-tus- modo, rūs-ticus ; hin-c vōs,
18 vōs hin-c mūtātīs- dis-cēdite par-tibus. ēja !
    quid- stātis-?" nōlin-t. at-quī licet es-se beātīs-.
20 quid- causae est, meritō quīn il-līs jūpiter am-bās-
    īrātus- buc-cās in-flet-? neque sē fore pos-thāc
22 tam- facilem- dīcat-, vōtīs ut praebeat aurem ?

                                    HOR. *Sat.* i. 1—22.

E.

Dedication of the Odes to Maecēnas.

See pp. 73. 101*.

    maecēnās, atavīs ēdite rēgibus,
2 ō et- praesidium et- dul-ce decus- meum-,

    sun-t quōs- cur-riculō pulvere^m⏑olym-picum-
4 col-lēgis-se juvat-, mētáque fer-vidīs
    ēvītāta rotīs- pal-máque nōbilis-
6 ter-rārum- dominōs- ēvehit ad- deōs-.
    mē doc-tāru^m⏑hederae praemia fron|tium-
8 dīs- mis-cen-t superīs- ; mē gelidum- nemus
    nym-phārúmque levēs- cum- satyrīs- chorī
10 sēcer-nun-t populō, sī neque tibiās
    euter-pē cohibet-, nec- polyhym-nia
12 les-bōum- refugit- ten-dere bar-biton.
    quod- sī mē lyricīs- vātibus īn-seris,
14 sub-līmī- feriam- sīdera ver-tice.

                    HOR. *OOd.* i. I. I—6. 29—36.

F.

Leuconoë Recommended not to Peer into the Future.

See pp. 67. 73. 104.*

    tū nē quaesieris-, scīre nefās- ! quem- mihi, quem- tibi
2 fīnem- dī dederin-t, leuconoē ; nec- babylōniōs-
    ten-tāris- numerōs.   ut- melius-, quic-quid erit-, patī !
4 seu plūrēs hiemēs-, seu tribuit- jūpiter ul-timam-,
    quae nunc op-positīs dēbilitat- pūmicibus- mare
6 tyr-rhēnum-: sapiàs-, vīna liquēs, et- spatiō brevī
    spēm- lon-gam- resecēs-. dum- loquimur-, fūgerit in-vida
8 aetās- ; car-pe diem-, quam- minimum- crēdula pos-terō.

                    HOR. *OOd.* i. II.

G.

While Ponticus writes Heroics, Propertius keeps to Erotics.

See pp. 74. 105*.

    dum- tibi cadmēae dīcun-tur-, pon-tice, thēbae,
2 ar-máque frāter-nae tris-tia mīlitiae.

at-que, ita sim- fēlīx-, prīmō con-ten-dis Homērō,
4   sin-t modo fāta tuīs- mol-lia car-minibus- !
nōs, ut- con-svēmus-, nōs-trōs agitāmus amōrēs,
6   at-que aliquid- dūram- quaerimus in- dominam- ;
nec- tan-tuᵐ in-geniō, quan-tum- servīre dolōrī
8   cōgor, et aetātis- tem-pora dūra querī.

PROP. *Eleg.* 7, 1—8.

H.

Pēnelopē writes to Ulixes.

See pp. 74. 105*.

han-c tua pēnelope len-tō tibi mit-tit, ulix-e,
2   nīl- mihi res-crībās, at-tamen ip-se venī.
trōja jacet- cer-tē, danaïs in-vīsa puel-līs- :
4   vix- priamus- tan-tī tōtáque trōja fuit.
o utinam- tun-c quum- lacedaemona clas-se petēbat
6   ob-rutus īn-sānīs es-set adul-ter aquīs- !
nōn ego dēser-tō jacuis-sem- frīgida lec-tō,
8   nec- quererer- tardōs īre relic-ta diēs ;
nec- mihi, quaeren-tī spatiōsam- fal-lere noc-tem-,
10   las-sāret viduās pen-dula tēla manūs.

Ov. *Hēr.* 1, 1—10.

I.

Hymn to Phoebus and Dianā.

See pp. 68. 74. 106*.

phoebe syl-vārúm-que poten-s diāna,
2   lūcidum- coelī decus, ō colen-dī
sem-per et- cul-tī, date quae precāmur-
4   tem-pore sac-rō

quō sybil-līnī monuēre ver-sūs
6 virginēs- lec-tās puerō's-que cas-tōs-
dīs, quibus- sep-tem- placuē're col-lēs,
8   dīcere car-men.
haec- jovem- sen-tīre deō's-que cun-ctōs
10 spēm- bonam- cer-tám-que domum- repor-tō,
doc-tus et- phoebī chorus et- diānae,
12   dīcere laudēs.
         HOR. *Carm. Saec.* 1—S. 73—76.

K.

The "*Just*" Man.

See pp. 25. 74. 75. 106*.

jus-tu^m‿et tenācem- prōpositī virum-
2 nōn cīviu^m‿ar-dor- prāva juben-tium-,
nōn vul-tus īn-stan-tis- tyran-nī
4   men-te quatit- solidā ; neque‿auster-,
dux- in-quiētī tur-bidus had-riae,
6 nec- ful-minan-tis- magna jovis- manus-,
sī frac-tus il-lābātur or-bis
8   im-pavidum- ferien-t ruīnae.
         HOR. *OOd.* iii. 3, 1—8.

L.

The Usurer's Anticipated Country Pleasures.

See pp. 42. 68. 77*. 107*.

beātus il-le, quī procul- negō-tiīs
2   ut- pris-ca gen-s mor-tālium-,
pater-na rūra būbus ēx-er-cet suīs-
4   solūtus om-nī foenere ;
neque‿ēx-citātur- clas-sicō mīles- trucī,
6   neque‿hor-ret īrātum- mare,

forúm-que vītat et- super-ba civium-
8   potentiōrum- līmina.
libet- jacēre modo sub an-tīquā ῑlice,
10   modo in- tenācī grāmine.
at- quum- tonan-tis an-nus hīber-nus- jovis
12   im-brēs nivē's-que com-parat,
aut trūdit ācrēs hin-c et hin-c multā cane
14   aprōs in ob-stan-tēs plagās ;
aut amite lēvī rāra ten-dit- rētia,
16   tur-dīs edācibus- dolōs ;
pavidúm-que lepore^m et ad-venam- laqueō gruem-,
18   jūcun-da cap-tat- praemia.
haec ubi locūtus- foenerātor al-fius,
20   jam-jam- futūrus- rūs-ticus,
om-nem- red^agit īdibus- pecūniam- ;
22   quaerit- calen-dīs- pōnere.

HOR. *Ep.* 2, 1—8. 23—24. 29—36. 67—70.

M.

Natural Melody as shewn by Latin Accent.

See pp. 8 note, 72. 73. 87. 108*. 109*.

es-t aute^m in- dīcen-dō etiam- quidam- can-tus ob-scūrior.
2   in-quō il-lud etiam- notan-dum- mihi vidētur ad- studium-
·per-sequen-dae svāvitātis in- vōcibus.   ip-sa enim- nātūra,
4   quasi modulārētur hominu^m ōrātiōne^m, in om-nī ver-bō posuit
acūtam- vōcem-, nec ūnā plūs-, nec ā pos-trēmā syl-labā cītrā
6   ter-tiam- : quō magis-nātūram- duce^m ad aurium- volup-tātem-
sequātur in-dus-tria.   āc-vōcis quidem- bonitās op-tan-da est.
8   nōn est eni^m in- nōbīs-, sed-trac-tātiō at-que ūsus in- nōbis.
er-gō il-le prin-cep-s variābit et- mūtābit ; om-nēs sonōrum-,
10   tu^m in-ten-den-s, tum- remit-ten-s, per-sequētur- gradūs.—CIC.
OOrātor. §§ 57—9.

N.

*Natural Feeling of Uneducated People for Long and Short
Quantities, and High and Low Pitch.*

See pp. 2 note, 9 note, 79. 109*.

in- ver-sū quidem- theātra tōta ēx-clāman-t sī fuit ūnā syl-
2 labā brevior aut lon-gior.   nec vērō mul-titūdō pedēs- nōvit,
nec ul-lōs- numerōs- tenet : nec il-lud-, quod of-fen-dit, aut
4 cūr, aut in- quō of-fen-dat, in-tel-ligit : et- tamen om-nium-
lon-gitūdinuᵐ et- brevitātuᵐ īn- sonīs-, sīcut acūtārum- gravium-
6 que vōcum- jūdiciuᵐ ip-sa nātūra, in auribus- nōstrīs- col-
locāvit.— Cɪᴄ. *OOrātor.* § 173.

O.

*Quantitative Rhythm in Prose, and the Resemblance of Greek Lyrics
and Latin Comic Sēnāriī to Prose Rhythms.*

See pp. 7. 9. 20. 79. 109*.

es-se er-gō in ōrātiōne numerum- quen-dam- nōn es-t dif-
2 ficile cog-nos-cere.   jūdicat enim- sen-sus : in- quō inīquuᵐ
est, quod ac-cidit-, nōn cog-noscere, sī, cūr id ac-cidat-, re-
4 perīre nequeāmus.   neque eniᵐ ip-se ver-sus- ratiōne es-t cog-
nitus-, sed- nātūrā at-que sen-sū, quem- dīmen-sa ratiō docuit-,
6 quid ac-ciderit.   ita notātiō nātūrae et animad-versiō peperit
ar-tem-.   sed in- ver-sibus- rēs es-t aper-tior- : quan-quaᵐ etiaᵐ
8 ā modīs- quibus-dam- can-tū remōtō, solūta es-se videātur ōrātiō.
max-imē'que in op-timō quōque eōrum- poētārum-, quī λυρικοὶ
10 ā graecīs- nōminan-tur- : quōs cum- can tū spoliāveris-, nūda
paene remanet ōrātiō.   quōrum- similia sun-t quaedaᵐ etiaᵐ
12 apud- nos-trōs, quae, nisi cum- tībīcen ac-ces-sit, ōrātiōnī sun-t
solūtae simil-lima.   at- cōmicōrum- sēnāriī prop-ter- similitū-
14 dinem- ser-mōnis sīc saepe sun-t ab-jec-tī ut- nōn-nun-quam-
vix in hīs numerus et- ver-sus in-tel-ligī possit.   quō es-t ad
16 in- venien-dum- dif-ficilior in ōrātiōne numerus-, quaᵐ in-
ver-sibus.—Cɪᴄ. *OOrātor.* §§ 183—4.

P.

Oratorical Effect of the Rhythmic Collocation of Words in Prose.

See pp. 9. 18. 26. 65. 79. 109*.

· · · · "per-solūtas." dīchoıē-us-. nihil enim ad- rēm,
2 ēx-trēma il-la, lon-ga sit an brevis. [quiā pos-trēma syl-laba
brevis an- longa sit, nē in-ver-sū quidem- rēfert. § 217] dēin-
4 de, "patris- dīc-tum- sapien-s, temeritās fīliī com-probāvit."
hōc dīchoreō tan-tus- clāmor- conciōnis ēx-citātus es-t, ut ad-
6 mīrābile es-set. quaerō, nōn-ne id- numerus ef-fēcerit-? verbōrum or-dinem im-mūtā. fac- sīc-, "com-probāvit fīliī teme-
8 ritās"; jam- nihil erit, et-sī "temeritās" ēx tribus- brevibus
et- lon-gā es-t : quem Aris-totelēs ut op-timum- probat, ā quō
10 dis-sen-tiō. at eadem- ver-ba, eadem- sen-ten-tia, animō
is-tuc- satis es-t, auribus- nōn- satis.—CIC. *O Orātor.* § 214—5.

Q.

*On Running Words together, Slurred Vowels, Open and Gating
Vowels, and the Poetic Use of Open Vowels.*

See pp. 16 note, 19. 36. 42. 53. 55. 79. 110*.

ut in- legen-dō oculus, sīc animus in- dī-cen-dō prōspiciet-
2 quid- sequātur, nē ēx-trēmōrum- ver-bōrum- cum īn-sequen-
tibus- prīmīs- con-cur-sus, aut hiul-cās- vōcēs ef-ficiat aut as-
4 perās-. quam-vīs enim- svāvēs- gravēs-que sen-ten-tiae, tamen-
si in-con-ditīs- ver-bīs ef-ferun-tur, of-fen-den-t aurēs; quārum
6 es-t jūdicium- super-bis-simum-. quod- quidem- Latīna lin-gua
sīc ob-ser-vat-, nēmō ut- tam- rūs-ticus sit-, quīn- vōcālēs-
8 nōlit- con-jun-gere. . . . . . sed- graecī vīderin-t ; nōbīs-, ne
sī cupiāmus- quidem-, dis-trahere vōcēs- con-cēditur. in-dican-t

10 ōrātiōnēs il-lae ip-sae hor-ridulae catōnis: in-dican-t em-nēs-
    poētae, praeter eōs-, quī ut- ver-sum- faceren-t, saepe hiāban-t:
12 ut en-nius semel-; "scīpio in-vic-te," et- quidem- nōs: "hōc-
    motū radian-tis etēsiae in- vada pon-tī." hōc idem- nōs-trī
14 saepius- nōn tulis-sen-t, quod- graecī laudāre etiam- solen-t.—
    Cɪc. *OOrātor.* § 150. 152. (See also § 153—162.)

See hiatuses in Ramsay's Prosody, p. 115, where he quotes
from Virgil, the hiatus being indicated by a dash :—

Amphīōn Dircaeus in Actaeō—Aracynthō.

Ec. ii. 24.

addam cērea prūna—honōs erit huic quoque pōmō.

Ec. ii. 53.

et sūcus pecorī—et lac subdūcitur agnīs.

Ec. iii. 6.

et, longum, formōse valē, vale—inquit, Iōla.

(the *ē* in the second *valē* shortened,) *Ec.* iii. 79.

stant et jūniperī—et castaneae—hirsūtae.

Ec. vii. 53.

crēdimus, ān qui—amant, ipsī sibi somnia fingunt.

(the *ī* in *quī* shortened,) *Ec.* viii. 108.

et vēra incessū patuit dea—ille ubi mātrem.

Aen. i. 405.

insulae—īoniō in magnō, quās dīra celaenō.

(the *ae* in *insulae* shortened, but *ō* in *īoniō* slurred, which word,
but for the necessity of verse, "ut versum faceret," would have been
īōniō, with the first short and second long,)

Aen. iii. 211.

nōmen et arma locum servant ; te—amīce nequīvī.

(the *ē* in *tē* shortened,) *Aen.* vi. 507.

Ramsay quotes also many other passages from Catullus, Virgil,
Horace (OOd. i, 28, 24 ; ii, 20, 13 ; Ep. 5, 100, not in *Sat.*,
except the passage with *num*, suprà p. 65, where he adds the conjecture "coctōve num adest,") Propertius, Ovid, among Augustan
writers ; shewing that the practice was not uncommon, and justifying
Cicero's remark, (Q. 11.)

R.

The Story of Gracchus's Piper and its Theory.

See pp. 20. 72. 79. 111*.

quid ad aurēs- nōs-strās et ac-tiōnis- svāvitātem-, quid es-t
2 vicis-si-tūdine, et varietāte, et com-mūtātiōne ap-tius? itaque
īdem- grac-chus-, (quod- potēs audīre, catule, ēx licīnō clien-te
4 tuō, lit-terātō homini, quem- ser-vum- sibi īl-le habuit ad
manum-), cum ebur-neolā solitus est habēre fis-tulā quī stāret
6 oc-cul-tē pos-t ip-sum- cum- con-tiōnārētur-, perītum hominem-,
quī īn-flāret- celeriter eum- so-num-, quō il-lum aut remis-sum
8 ēxcitāret aut ā con-ten-tiōne revocāret.
audīvī, mēher-culē, in-quit catulus, et saepe sum ad-mīratus
10 hominis- cum- dīligen-tiam- tum etiam- doc-trīnam et scien-tiam.
ego vērō, in-quit- cras-sus, āc doleō quidem il-lōs virōs in
12 eam- fraudem in rēpūblicā es-se dēlap-sōs . . . .
mit-te, ob-secrō, in-quit-, cras-se, jūlius, ser-mōnem is-tum,
14 et te ad- grac-chī fis-tulam- refer : cūjus ego nōn-dum- plānē
ratiōnem in-tel-ligō.
16 in om-nī vōce, in-quit cras-sus, es-t quid-dam- medium-, sed-
suum- cuique vōcī. hinc gradātim ascen-dere vōcem ūtile et
18 suāve es-t. nam ā prin-cipiō clāmāre, agres-te quid-dam es-t,
et il-lud idem ad- fir-man-dum est vōcem- salūtāre. dēin-de
20 es-t quid-dam- con-ten-tiōnis ēx-trēmum-, quod- tamen īn-feriūs
es-t quam acūtis-simus- clāmor-, quō tē fis-tula prōgredī nōn
22 sinet, et- tamen ab ip-sā con-ten-tiōne revocābit. es-t item-
con-trā quid-da m in remis-siōne grāvis-simum-, quōque tan-
24 quam- sonōrum- gradibus- dēscen-ditur. haec varietās, et hīc-
per om-nes- sonōs- vōcis cur-sus, et- sē tuēbitur, et ac-tiōnī af-
26 feret- svāvitātem-. sed fis-tulātōrem- domī relin-quētis, sen-
sum hūjus con-suē-tūdinis vōbīs-cum ad- forum- dēferētis.—
Cic. *Dē OOrātōre.* lib. iii. §§ 225—228.

S.

Opening of " Jerusalem Delivered," an Example of Slurred Vowels and Unwritten Assimilated Consonants.

See pp. 37. 52. 54. 55*. 113.

-canto l'armi pietose‿, e'l capitano
2   -che'l gran sepolcro liberò -di cristo.
-molto‿egli‿oprò -col senno‿, e -con la mano ;
4   -molto soffrì -nel glorioso‿acquisto ;
e‿invan l'inferno‿a -lui s'oppose‿, e‿invano
6   -s'armò -d'asia‿e -di libia‿il popol misto ;
-che‿il -ciel gli diè -favore‿, e -sotto‿ai santi
8   segni ridusse‿i suoi compagni‿erranti.

o musa tu, che di caduchi‿allori
10   non circondi la fronte‿in elicona,
ma su nel cielo‿infra‿i beati cori
12   hai di stelle‿immortali‿aurea corona ;
tu spira‿al petto mio celesti‿ardori,
14   tu rischiara‿il mio canto‿, e tu perdona
se‿intesso fregi‿al ver, s'adorno‿in parte
16   d'altri diletti che de' tuoi le carte.

TASSO. *Ger. Lib.* i. 1—16.

K

INDEX OF AUTHORS CITED.

THE numbers in parentheses refer to the passage in the works of the author cited. The other numbers give the page in this tract. An added *n* refers to a note.

www.ingramcontent.com/pod-product-compliance
Lightning Source LLC
Chambersburg PA
CBHW030602270326
41927CB00007B/1011